An Instant Guide to
WEATHER

*A guide to recognizing different weather
phenomena and understanding their causes.
Illustrated throughout in full color.*

ELEANOR LAWRENCE

ILLUSTRATED BY
BORIN VAN LOON

GRAMERCY BOOKS
NEW YORK

This 2000 edition is published by Gramercy Books™,
an imprint of Random House Value Publishing, Inc.,
201 East 50th Street, New York, New York 10022.

Gramercy Books™ and colophon are trademarks of
Random House Value Publishing, Inc.

Random House
New York • Toronto • London • Sydney • Auckland
http://www.randomhouse.com/

Printed and bound in Singapore

Library of Congress Cataloging-in-Publication Data

Forey, Pamela.
    An instant guide to weather : a guide to recognizing different weather
phenomena and understanding their causes / Pamela Forey and Cecilia
Fitzsimons.
        p. cm.
    Originally published: London : Malcolm Saunders Pub., c1992.
    Includes index.
    ISBN 0-517-20833-4
        1. Meteorology—Observers' manuals. I. Fitzsimons, Cecilia. II. Title.

 QC871.4 .F67 2000
 551.6—dc21

                                                            99-050242

8 7 6 5 4 3 2

Contents

Introduction

The weather affects us all, but we rarely stop to consider its causes until extreme weather conditions inconvenience people or place them in danger. Hurricanes, floods and droughts hit the headlines as they bring tragedy to thousands of people. They are a reminder of the power of the forces that generate the weather, which most of us thankfully experience in a less dreadful guise. The weather is one of those things we cannot control. The best we can do is to study it carefully so that we can be forewarned about what it will bring.

Following the day-to-day changes in the weather and getting to know your local conditions can be a fascinating and rewarding pastime. This book will help you recognize different types of weather and weather phenomena, and will explain how they are caused. It will help you get started on keeping a record of the weather, and as your knowledge increases you will be able to recognize for yourself the local signs that the weather is changing – for better or worse.

How to use this book

The book is divided into eight sections: **The Atmosphere**; **Weather Systems**; **Clouds**; **Precipitation (Rain, Snow,** and **Hail)**; **Winds**; **Optical and Atmospheric Phenomena**; **Climate**; and **Observation and Forecasting**. Each section is indicated by a different color band at the top of each page together with an identification symbol. In the section **The Atmosphere** some basic information is given to help you understand how weather is produced; in **Weather Systems**, the main types of weather systems and their associated weather are illustrated and explained; the section **Clouds** explains how clouds are formed and illustrates many of the different types; in **Precipitation** we explain how rain, hail and snow are produced; the section on **Winds** deals with winds and phenomena such as hurricanes that generate strong winds; the section on **Optical and Atmospheric Phenomena** illustrates some of the wonderful sights you can see in the sky; a selection of world climates are defined in the section **Climates**; and the final section **Observation and Forecasting** provides advice on making your own weather observations. Several sections also include weather conditions and types of air pollution relevant to the main section topic.

The Atmosphere

This section provides some background information on the atmosphere and the properties of air that are necessary to understand how weather is formed. Also included here are pages on the "greenhouse effect" and on the "holes" in the ozone layer.

Weather Systems

This section deals with the main larger-scale influences on our weather, including air masses, fronts, and high- and low-pressure systems, and shows how they are depicted on a weather map.

Clouds

Here you will find descriptions and illustrations of the main types of clouds and how they are formed. Also included are some special clouds that occur in particular situations. Fog, dew and frost are also covered here as their formation is very similar to that of clouds, except that they are produced at ground level.

Precipitation (Rain, Hail, and Snow)

This section includes a description of the water cycle and illustrates how rain, hail, and snow are produced, and some of the weather conditions associated with them.

Winds

In this section the nature and classification of winds are described, as well as some local winds and weather phenomena with which winds are associated, such as hurricanes, tornadoes, and waterspouts.

Optical and Atmospheric Phenomena

This section describes and illustrates how light causes optical atmospheric phenomena like rainbows, halos, and coronas. It also covers thunderstorms, lightning, and the aurora.

Climate

This section gives a map of world climates and describes eight different types.

Observation and Forecasting

This section explains how weather forecasts are produced and some of the instruments you need to make your own weather observations. Examples show how basic information is used by meterologists in different ways. Charts of the upper air pressure help forecast surface conditions, while information gathered over many years makes it possible to give the average expected conditions for different weather features for a particular location in any particular month. Further information on weather can be found via the US National Weather Service's web site at :

http://www.nws.noaa.gov

Now you are ready to use this book. If you wish, you can study the weather in your own local area from the comfort of an armchair in front of the window. But take a trip out from time to time, especially in changeable weather, to where you can see the whole sweep of the sky. And remember to take this book with you on outings to places where the weather is different from that at home – to the coast, perhaps, or the mountains. Have a fine day!

Specimen page

Symbol and band color denote section

Name of topic

Illustration

Descriptive panel

CLOUD STREETS

Over open country **cumulus** clouds often line up in a row, which is called a cloud street. These formations are sometimes the result of a succession of clouds being generated in the moist air carried upwards by a thermal and then moving downwind. On a sunny day over a flat uniform surface, regular parallel streets of clouds may be formed, extending into the distance as far as the eye can see. These are the result of the pattern of updrafts and downdrafts created by general heating of the land and the direction of the breeze. On satellite photographs large areas of cloud streets are often spotted over the seas.

51

What is Weather?

Our weather is the outcome of the unique combination of the type of atmosphere our planet possesses, its abundant water, and our distance from the Sun. A little nearer and we might be permanently shrouded in stifling clouds; farther away, all water would be permanently frozen.

The powerful force driving the weather is ultimately the Sun's energy. This sets the air in the atmosphere moving. Solar energy is also stored and released when water is converted from liquid to vapor or ice and back again. As the air responds to changes in temperature by becoming lighter or heavier, wetter or drier, clouds are formed, rain falls, air pressure changes, and winds blow.

The weather we experience at any particular place and time is the result of the prevailing conditions in the layer of the atmosphere nearest the Earth's surface. All our weather is generated in the troposphere, this densest and lowest part of the atmosphere. Conditions here vary from hour to hour throughout the day, from day to day, from place to place, and from season to season as the Earth, tilted on its axis, makes its annual journey around the Sun. Different parts of the Earth experience different patterns of weather throughout the year, and this is their climate.

For everyday purposes we usually only need to describe the weather as fine, fair, bad, or foul. Meteorologists, however, must record and describe prevailing weather conditions more precisely, in terms of a combination of temperature, air pressure, humidity, cloud type and cover, visibility, precipitation, and wind speed and direction. The atmosphere is such a complicated physical machine that in most places, the weather it will generate on any particular day in the future is still almost completely unpredictable for more than a few days ahead. Using the knowledge gathered from over a hundred years of detailed weather observations, from satellite observations, and from powerful computer models of atmospheric behavior, short-term weather forecasts are now usually very accurate. But whether the day of the summer party planned long in advance will be warm and sunny, or cold and rainy is still very much a matter of chance, and is something we cannot control.

Glossary

adiabatic refers to warming and cooling of air by the effects of expansion and compression under the influence of pressure alone, without any external sources of heating or cooling.

altitude height above sea level.

condensation conversion of water vapor into liquid water.

condensation point the temperature at which water starts to condense out of air. It varies with the humidity of the air.

continental refers to lands away from the oceans and whose climates are not subject to the moderating influence of the sea.

convection the vertical movement of air or water as a result of temperature changes.

dew point see **condensation point**.

diffraction the bending of light around obstacles such as air molecules and water droplets.

evaporation the conversion of water from liquid to vapor.

inversion a layer of cool air trapped by warmer air above it.

humidity refers to the water content of the air.

isobars lines on the weather chart that join points of equal surface pressure.

lee, leeward the side of a mountain range or other obstruction facing away from the prevailing wind.

maritime refers to countries bordering the oceans and whose climates are influenced by the moderating effects of the ocean.

meteorology the study of the weather and the atmosphere.

midlatitudes latitudes between around 30° and 70° N or S.

precipitation rain, snow, or hail.

refraction the bending of light as it passes from one transparent medium, e.g. air, into another of different density, e.g. water.

saturated refers to air holding the maximum amount of water vapor it can at that temperature, i.e. it has a relative humidity of 100%. The **saturation point** of air is the temperature at which it becomes saturated.

stable refers to air in which there is little vertical movement. If air is forced to rise in a stable environment it will soon become cooler than its surroundings and will sink back towards the surface. Stability depends in complex ways on temperature and humidity; as a general rule air that is cool near the surface and warmer higher up is generally stable. See also **unstable**.

stratosphere the layer of the atmosphere immediately above the troposphere.

supercooled refers to water droplets that have cooled to below freezing point but do not freeze because of their small size.

tropical lying between latitudes 23° 27' N (Tropic of Cancer) and 23° 27' S (Tropic of Capricorn), between which the Sun is directly overhead at some time of the year.

tropopause the boundary between troposphere and stratosphere.

troposphere the lowest and densest layer of the atmosphere; the layer in which our weather occurs.

turbulence irregularities in wind speed and direction.

unstable refers to air in which there is a tendency for vertical movement. If air is forced to rise in an unstable environment it will soon become or remain warmer than its surroundings and continue to rise. Instability depends in complex ways on temperature and humidity; as a general rule, air that is warm near the surface and much colder higher up is generally unstable. See also **stable**.

The Atmosphere

The atmosphere envelops the Earth in a protective blanket of gases, extending thousands of miles out into space. This envelope is densest at the Earth's surface, rapidly thinning out with height. Without an atmosphere the Earth would be subject to the extremes of temperature experienced by the airless Moon; there would be no weather, and there would be no life. The atmosphere is divided into several distinct layers with different temperature gradients, compositions, and properties. Most of our weather is formed in the lowest layer, the troposphere, which contains 90% of all the atmosphere by mass. This is the layer influenced by the temperature and topography of the Earth's surface. The air in the troposphere is constantly in motion, stirred and mixed by the transfer of heat from the sun-warmed Earth. The **temperature**, **pressure**, and **humidity** of air in the troposphere are continually changing and it is these changes that make our weather.

A thin boundary layer – the tropopause – divides the troposphere from the stratosphere and marks the farthest extent of the Earth's influence on atmospheric temperature. Air temperature decreases with altitude up to the tropopause, where it stops decreasing. The tropopause forms a ceiling on our weather and the stratosphere above is free of cloud and relatively calm. Airplanes often fly at or just above the tropopause to avoid clouds and turbulence. The height of the tropopause above the surface varies from around 5 miles at the poles to around 11 miles over the tropics. Within the stratosphere lies the **ozone layer**. This absorbs much of the ultraviolet radiation from the Sun, shielding the Earth's surface from its harmful effects.

Composition of the air

Air in the troposphere consists mainly of nitrogen (76%) and oxygen (21%), with small amounts of carbon dioxide (around 0.03%), water vapor (1 to 4%), argon and hydrogen. As far as weather is concerned, the most important ingredient is water vapor. This evaporates into the air from the Earth's surface, condenses into **clouds**, and is returned to the Earth as **rain** and **snow**. Air also contains minute particles of dust and salt; these provide surfaces on which water droplets condense. The air now also contains chemical pollutants, many of which are formed as we burn fossil fuels in our homes, factories, and cars. These contribute to the haze and **smog** above some cities.

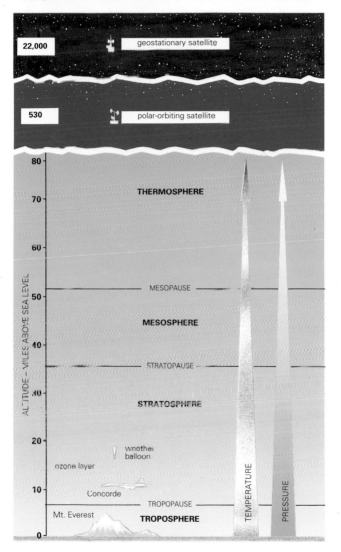

22,000 — geostationary satellite

530 — polar-orbiting satellite

ALTITUDE - MILES ABOVE SEA LEVEL

80 —

70 — **THERMOSPHERE**

60 —

50 — MESOPAUSE

40 — **MESOSPHERE**

STRATOPAUSE

30 —

STRATOSPHERE

20 —

weather balloon

ozone layer

10 —

Concorde

TROPOPAUSE

Mt. Everest   **TROPOSPHERE**

0 —

TEMPERATURE

PRESSURE

THE OZONE LAYER

OZONE CONCENTRATION IN THE STRATOSPHERE

normal

low

ANTARCTICA

In the stratosphere there is a layer of ozone molecules (O_3) which is thickest between 9 and 15 miles above the Earth's surface. Ozone is continually being formed from oxygen (O_2) by the action of sunlight and decays slowly back into oxygen. The ozone layer blankets out most of the Sun's ultraviolet rays, protecting life on Earth from the harmful effects of this radiation. Ultraviolet radiation causes mutations; even with the low levels reaching us now, excessive exposure to sunlight can cause skin cancers, especially in light-skinned people. Some years ago, scientists found that the ozone layer had thinned by as much as a half in places. These "holes" in the layer appear above the Antarctic in October (illustration) and the Arctic in spring. At the same time it was found that chlorofluorocarbons (CFCs), chemicals that were commonly used as propellants in aerosols and as refrigerants, were powerful destroyers of ozone and might be contributing to the thinning of the layer. Light acts on CFCs to release chlorine, which in turn reacts with ozone, splitting it into oxygen and oxides of chlorine. The manufacture and use of CFCs is now decreasing.

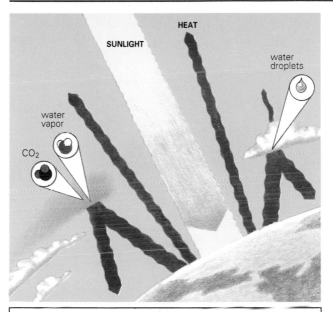

As you go farther away from the Earth's surface the air in the troposphere gets colder. This is because air in this layer of the **atmosphere** is not warmed directly by the Sun, but by contact with the surface of the Earth. The outermost layers of the atmosphere are intensely hot, as they absorb X-rays and other very short wavelengths from the solar radiation. But most solar radiation that reaches the Earth's surface is in the visible light wavelengths, which pass through air without being absorbed. Light is absorbed by the surface, which warms up and emits radiation as heat (the infrared wavelengths). This warms the air above the surface as the molecules of water vapor (H_2O) and carbon dioxide (CO_2) in air absorb radiation in these wavelengths. They also re-radiate energy as heat. If all the heat radiated by the Earth were lost upwards into space the Earth would be a much colder place. But most heat is directed back towards the Earth's surface from the bases of clouds and from the air itself – the **greenhouse effect** – so that the overall heat budget is balanced. The average temperature at the surface is 59°F, but temperature varies enormously from place to place.

THE GREENHOUSE EFFECT

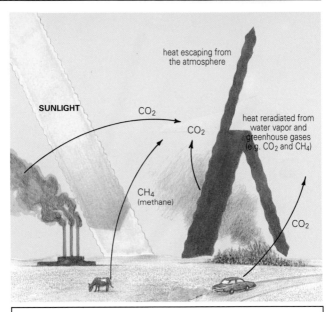

The **atmosphere** allows visible light through, but water vapor, carbon dioxide (CO_2), and some other natural and man-made gases in the atmosphere (the "greenhouse gases") absorb much of the heat emitted by the Earth and re-radiate it back to the surface. This is popularly known as the greenhouse effect, and is important in regulating the Earth's temperature. The amount of carbon dioxide in the atmosphere is small (0.03%), but has been rising steadily over the past century as the result of massive burning of fossil fuels (gas, oil, and coal) in the industrial world. This puts more carbon dioxide into the atmosphere than is currently being removed by photosynthesis into long-term storage in forests. Since 1958, for example, atmospheric CO_2 has increased by 11%. Many scientists now believe that an unchecked increase in CO_2 and other greenhouse gases could contribute to a serious rise in the Earth's surface temperature in the future. It is estimated that a doubling of atmospheric CO_2 could lead to a rise of between 3 and 10° F. Such warming could change climates drastically and might even melt polar ice, raising sea level around the world and threatening many centers of population.

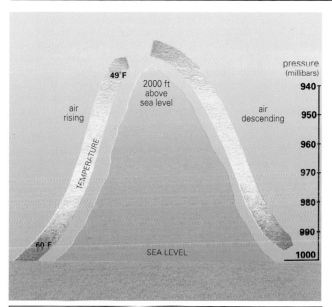

The mass of **atmosphere** exerts pressure, averaging 1013 millibars (mb) at the Earth's surface. Pressure at sea level may rise or fall by up to 50 mb in a day, but we do not sense changes in pressure unless they occur very suddenly, as the pressure of air within our bodies rapidly equalizes to that outside. Air pressure decreases with height above the Earth as the atmosphere gets thinner. Near the surface, for the first 3000 feet or so, pressure falls at a rate of approximately 1 mb per 33 feet altitude and at a height of around 18,000 feet pressure averages 500 mb, half that at the surface. Horizontal differences in air pressure generate winds, as air flows from an area of high pressure into a low pressure area. The vertical decrease in pressure has very important effects on the properties of the air. Air that is forced to rise for any reason expands as the pressure exerted on it decreases. Expanding air cools down. Conversely, sinking air becomes compressed. Compressed air warms up. The warming and cooling of air by changes in pressure alone are known as adiabatic warming and cooling, and are important in many weather phenomena.

19

The General Circulation

The large-scale circulation of air in the troposphere is caused by the unequal heating of the surface of the globe. Temperature differences between the Equator and poles and between land and sea generate the great air movements that provide the framework for all our weather. Within latitudes 35° North and 35° South, the Earth's surface receives more radiation than it loses as heat, but at the poles it receives less than it loses (see diagram below). If heat were not continually transported polewards from the Equator, tropical regions would become hotter and polar regions colder. The atmosphere is one agent of this heat transfer; the other is the ocean. The global atmospheric circulation is extraordinarily complex and scientists do not yet understand it completely.

The general circulation produces the strong dependable winds that blow across the open oceans, such as the Trade Winds in the tropics and the prevailing westerlies further north and south (see **Global Winds**). At the Equator itself, the rising air creates the windless doldrums. The general flow of air is eastwards across the Pacific and the northern Atlantic. The general eastward trend of the weather becomes disturbed over continents such as North America, where mountains, valleys, deserts, and forests influence local and regional weather.

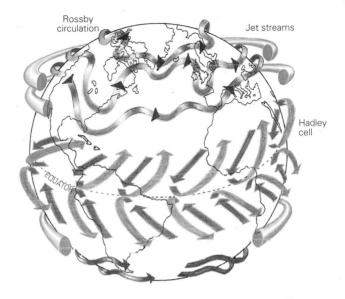

Warm air rising at the Equator, where most solar radiation is received, is carried away southwards and northwards and replaced at the surface by cooler air moving in. The warm air moving away from the Equator starts to cool and descend at around 30°N and 30°S. This simple circulation, called a Hadley cell, is deflected to the right in the Northern Hemisphere and to the left in the Southern Hemisphere as a result of the Earth's eastwards rotation, giving rise at the surface to the Trade Winds (see **Global Winds**). Farther towards the poles the circulation grows more complicated. Undulating streams of air (Rossby waves) travel around the globe from west to east, mixing and stirring the atmosphere and bringing warm air towards the poles and cold air towards the Equator. Sheets of cold air coming southward slide under sheets of warmer air moving northward. The surface winds in these latitudes are the prevailing westerlies. The jet streams are narrow ribbons of fast-moving wind also streaming eastwards, encircling the globe high above the surface at sharp discontinuities in temperature, helping to transfer heat between warm tropical air and cold polar air.

Global Currents

The other agents of heat transfer between Equator and poles are the ocean currents. Warm currents like the Gulf Stream in the North Atlantic and the Brazil Current in the South Atlantic flow polewards from the Equator, and cold currents like the icy Labrador Current off the eastern North American coast and the Humboldt Current along the Chilean and Peruvian coast carry cold water away from the poles. The map shows the main ocean currents in the Northern hemisphere winter. The small picture below shows how they change off India and southeast Asia with the monsoon winds in summer.

The great ocean currents have their origin in the surface winds that blow across the ocean. The Gulf Stream sweeps up the eastern North Atlantic and across to the Arctic as a result of the clockwise winds around the area of persistent high pressure located over the Azores.

Currents near continental coasts can influence the general climate and day-to-day weather. Summer fogs off Newfoundland, for example, are due to the cold Labrador Current meeting the warmer Gulf Stream. Warm currents can make an area milder than one would expect for the latitude, as air coming over the current is warmed and moistened. The warm North Atlantic Drift, the northern continuation of the Gulf Stream, keeps the coasts of Norway free of ice in winter, whereas the St Lawrence River across the Atlantic is blocked by ice.

EQUATOR

Humidity

As far as weather is concerned, water (H_2O) is the most important ingredient of the atmosphere. Air always contains some water vapor, on average between 1 and 4%, but the amount varies widely. Although water vapor is invisible, we can usually sense when air is moist or humid. Warm moist air makes us feel uncomfortable as it prevents sweat evaporating from our skins and cooling us. Cold moist air feels much more chilling than drier air at the same temperature. The amount of water in the air is known as its **humidity**. The maximum amount of water vapor that air can hold depends on the air temperature. Warm air can hold more water as vapor than can cold air. Air that is holding the maximum possible amount of water at a given temperature is said to be saturated.

Air temp (°C)	Saturation value (in grams water per cubic meter of air)
86°F	30.4
50°F	9.4
32°F	4.9
−4°F	1.0

Humidity is often expressed as relative humidity (R.H.). This is the percentage of water vapor the air is holding at a particular temperature compared with the maximum amount it could contain at that temperature. As air cools its relative humidity increases until it reaches 100% – saturation point. If it is cooled any further the vapor must start to condense out as droplets of water (see **Clouds**). We can see moisture condensing when we breathe out warm moist air into the cold air of a winter's day.

Absolute humidity = 7.27 grams of water vapor per cubic meter				
Temp	43°F	50°F	61°F	86°F
R.H.(%)	100	77	53	24

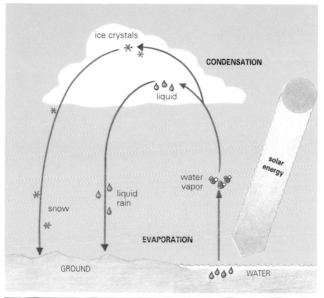

On our planet water can exist as a gas (water vapor), as a liquid, and as a solid (ice). Water is continually evaporating from the Earth's surface into the air where it is held as invisible water vapor which eventually condenses into tiny water droplets to form **clouds**. When condensation takes place in the highest and coldest reaches of the sky, clouds are made of ice crystals. Given the right conditions, clouds return the water to Earth again as rain or snow to complete the water cycle. Evaporation of liquid water to vapor, without a change in temperature, requires a large amount of energy that ultimately comes from the Sun. This energy becomes locked up in the water vapor and is released as latent heat of condensation when vapor condenses. The heat released when large masses of moist air condense helps to generate **cumulonimbus** thunderclouds and **hurricanes**.

When the **atmospheric pressure** at the Earth's surface is plotted, distinct areas of high and low pressure emerge. The areas change from day to day and from season to season, and each has its own distinctive weather patterns. The weather systems based on these areas of low and high pressure determine our day-to-day weather and can extend over thousands of square miles. Looking down on the Earth from space, the whirlpools and eddies of thick cloud indicate low-pressure systems (**cyclones**) – the "lows" or depressions of the **weather map**. Low-pressure systems generally bring unsettled or bad weather, ranging from a few light showers to a raging tropical **hurricane**. High-pressure areas (**anticyclones**), on the other hand, are usually associated with fine weather, especially in summer, but the situation is often more complicated. Large weather systems are generated as a result of the differences in temperature, pressure and humidity between different **air masses**. Where two air masses of different properties meet, a **front** is formed, usually accompanied by clouds and rain. Localized air movements create depressions along the front.

WEATHER MAP

This simplified weather chart, of the sort you will find in your newspapers, shows the disposition of areas of low and high pressure (**cyclones** and **anticyclones**) at the surface, with their associated fronts, over North America for a particular day in spring. Charts like these are compiled from data obtained from hundreds of meteorological stations. Points of equal atmospheric pressure are joined by thin lines called isobars, and are drawn here at intervals of 5 millibars. The thick lines represent the surface edges of fronts, estimated from the positions of low and high pressure areas.

▲▲ moving **cold front**

●● moving **warm front**

▲●▲ moving **occluded front**

▼▼ stationary front

— 1000 — isobars with surface pressure in millibars

The weather is largely determined by what the air above us is like. Is it warm or cold, moist or dry? Air over warm tropical seas, for example, will always be warmer and moister than air over cold polar regions. Over the oceans and continental interiors the air is quite uniform in its temperature and humidity in a horizontal direction. These large bodies of air are known as air masses. Air masses are often on the move, influencing weather in regions far away and becoming warmer or colder, wetter or drier, as they pass over different surfaces. The main types of air mass are: maritime polar (mP), continental polar (cP), maritime tropical (mT), and continental tropical (cT). In much simplified terms, mP air is cold and moist, cP air is cold and dry, mT air is warm and wet, whereas cT air is hot and dry. Strong **fronts** are formed where cold polar air and warm tropical air meet. cP air moving south is generally colder than the land it travels over; warming makes the air mass unstable, producing clouds and rain (or snow). Warm mT air moving north, in contrast, is usually hotter than the land surface and therefore, even though the air is moist, it produces little rain unless it hits cold air or is forced over a mountain range.

CANADIAN POLAR FRONT

ATLANTIC
POLAR FRONT
(summer)

cA | cP
mP | mI | cT

The United States east of the Rocky Mountains is influenced by cold air masses that develop over the forests and tundra of Canada and over the northern Atlantic, warm air that comes in from the Atlantic, and hot dry air that develops over the interior in the Southwest. Extremely cold arctic polar air (cA) sits over the ice cap. Very cold, dry continental polar air (cP) originates in northeastern and central Canada and moves southwards, most frequently along a southeasterly path that takes it over the Great Lakes, where it picks up moisture, and into the northeastern and central United States, bringing snow in winter. In winter it can move south as far as Florida. Cold, moist maritime polar (mP) air travels over the northeast, bringing rain. Further south, the weather is influenced by warm, moist maritime tropical air (mT) coming in from the Atlantic over the Caribbean and the Gulf of Mexico. The west coast is influenced by air flowing in from over the Pacific: cool mP air from the north, and warm mT air from the south. A hot, dry continental tropical air mass (cT) that forms over the interior of the Southwest also influences regions to the east. The illustration shows the general picture for summer.

FRONTS

When a warm air mass meets a cooler one, a distinct boundary – a **front** – is formed, often thousands of miles long. The warmer air along the front rises over the cooler air to give a boundary sloping up from the ground and separating warm air from cold. As the warm air rises it cools and a belt of cloud and rain (or snow) is formed. Strong fronts, separating air masses of markedly different temperatures, develop in northern latitudes where cold polar air meets warm tropical air. They are invariably accompanied by rain or snow, often with high winds, and herald a change in the weather as one air mass moves in to replace the other. Weaker fronts, separating air with similar properties, may pass unnoticed except for a slight drop in pressure. The front that most influences North American weather is the North Atlantic or Polar Front (see p. 29), which represents the boundary between cP air and warmer air to the south. In summer it generally remains far to the north, but in winter it can move far down into the US. Fronts may be stationary, but usually one air mass is moving, pushing the other along. There are three main types of front, each accompanied by a typical weather sequence (see **Cold Front**, **Warm Front**, and **Occluded Front**).

CYCLONES (DEPRESSIONS)

A cyclone or depression (the "Low" of the weather charts) is a distinct area of low pressure in the atmosphere, with pressure lowest at the center. It is maintained by air rising at the center of the low and being removed rapidly by high-level winds blowing away from the center. At surface level, air is drawn into the depression and is deflected around the center (see **Coriolis Effect**). Winds therefore blow counterclockwise around a depression in the Northern Hemisphere (clockwise in the Southern Hemisphere). High winds accompany lows when there is a steep pressure gradient from rim to center and air rushes into the depression. Cyclones are typically thousands of miles across and extend vertically throughout the troposphere (see p. 119). Low-pressure systems in the middle latitudes are associated with cloud and rain or snow as a result of condensation and precipitation from the rising and cooling air. Over tropical waters cyclones can develop into **hurricanes**. Cyclones often are generated along fronts such as the Polar Front in the northern latitudes (see **Occluded Fronts**). "Valleys" of low pressure are called troughs. See p. 27 for symbols.

ANTICYCLONES

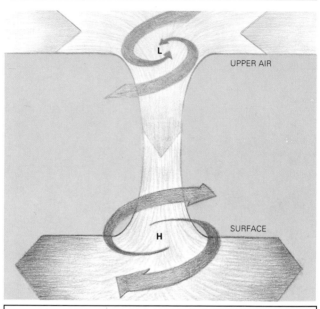

Anticyclones (the "Highs" of the weather charts) are systems of high pressure in the atmosphere, and can extend over vast areas. The air at the center of an anticyclone is descending towards the Earth's surface, becoming compressed and warmed as it sinks. At the surface, air flows outwards from the center of an anticyclone and is deflected as a result of the **Coriolis Effect**. Winds blow clockwise around an anticyclone in the Northern Hemisphere (counterclockwise in the Southern). The pressure gradient from the center outwards is rarely as steep as in a **cyclone** and winds in anticyclones are usually lighter. Anticyclones are often associated with fine sunny weather as clouds are less likely to form in the sinking warming air. Stationary "blocking anticyclones" cause the spells of fine but extreme weather experienced from time to time – heatwaves and droughts in summer and bitter cold in winter. Seasonal anticyclones develop in winter over the snow-covered interiors of continents as air is cooled, becomes denser and sinks. The highest surface pressure (1080mb) ever recorded came from the center of the winter "Siberian High."

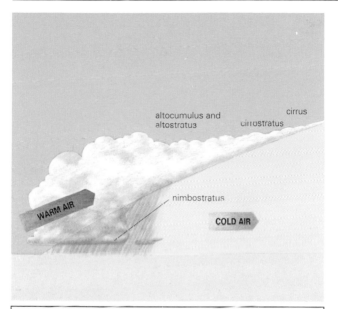

altocumulus and
altostratus

cirrus

cirrostratus

WARM AIR

nimbostratus

COLD AIR

Warm fronts (see **Weather map** for symbol) occur when warm air moves in to replace a cold air mass. The advancing warm air flows up and over the cold air to form a gently sloping boundary between warm and cool air. This may stretch as much as 600 miles ahead of the surface line of the front. Clouds condense in the rising, cooling air. A warm front is heralded some 48 hours before by **cirrus** clouds, the first sign of the warm air high above, and a fall in pressure. Cirrus gives way to **cirrostratus**. Mid-level **altostratus** clouds follow, giving a leaden overcast sky, or, if the warm air is unstable, a **cirrocumulus** "mackerel sky.' Dark low-based **nimbostratus** clouds precede the line of the front itself, bringing persistent rain or snow. The rainbelt can be from 15 to 200 miles wide and take 6 hours or more to pass, after which the pressure starts to rise. Warm fronts move fairly slowly, at around 15 miles per hour (mph). If the warm air is unstable, the front may be accompanied by **cumulonimbus** clouds, giving a mixture of steady rain, drizzle, and thunder showers. Warm fronts in depressions are often closely followed by a cold front (see **Occluded Front**).

COLD FRONT

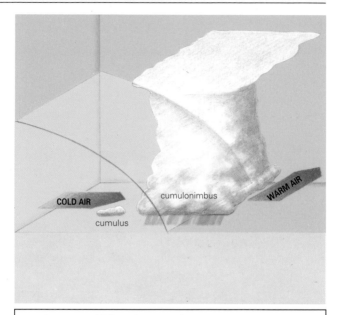

COLD AIR

cumulus

cumulonimbus

WARM AIR

An advancing cold front (see **Weather Map** for symbol) is typically accompanied by a fall in pressure, followed by heavy showers which clear rapidly to give colder brighter weather and rising air pressure. A cold front forms when a thick wedge of cold air pushes forward under a warm air mass. The warm air is forced sharply up and **cumulonimbus** clouds condense in the rapidly rising and cooling air. They give heavy, sometimes thundery, showers that do not last very long. Cold fronts usually travel faster than **warm fronts**, up to 25 to 30 mph compared to around 15 mph. They are also narrower and the whole front has usually passed over within 4 to 5 hours, hence the saying "rain before seven, fine before eleven." Cold fronts may be preceded by high **cirrus** clouds, but these often cannot be seen above the low clouds of the warm air mass and the thick rain-bearing clouds arrive without warning. Slower moving cold fronts give steadier rain from **nimbostratus** clouds mixed with the heavier showers from cumulonimbus clouds. Cold fronts often closely follow fronts embedded in depressions (see **Occluded Fronts**).

OCCLUDED FRONT

Occluded fronts (see **Weather Map** for symbol) are produced when a **cold front** catches up a **warm front**, and they typically form in midlatitude **cyclones** (depressions). In the Northern Hemisphere, cyclones develop along the front separating the northern cold air mass from warm air to the south (**1**) When the cold air pushes forward under the warmer air at some point (**2**), the front kinks, trapping a sector of warm air between the two arms (**3**). The leading arm becomes a warm front as the warm air in this sector is squeezed up and over the cold air ahead of it by the faster traveling cold front following it. An area of low pressure is formed around the "kink" as cold air moves rapidly away from it and warm air moves more slowly into it. The cold front usually moves about twice as fast as the warm front and eventually catches up with it (**4**), lifting all the warm air aloft and producing an **occluded front**. The persistent rain typical of a warm front is followed immediately by showers from the **cumulonimbus** clouds accompanying the cold front, without any intervening fine spell. Once the front has become occluded the depression ceases to grow and pressure starts to equalize.

RED SKY AT NIGHT

"Red sky at night, sailor's delight; red sky in morning, sailors take warning" is one piece of weather lore known throughout the world. The Chinese will tell you to "stay at home when the morning sky appears red, but look for a good day's travel when the evening clouds turn crimson." The saying is one of the more reliable pieces of folklore about the weather, at least in situations where **fronts** with their associated cloud and rain generally travel from west to east. Vividly colored skies are produced when the rising or setting Sun shines through a dry, hazy, and dusty atmosphere, conditions typical of anticyclonic air. Red skies in the east in the morning suggest that the fine weather has already passed over; any clouds illuminated by the rising Sun are likely to be the forerunners of an advancing front. A red sky in the west in evening is more hopeful. The dry air is on the way, bringing fine weather with it.

Clouds

Clouds are the easiest aspect of the weather to study. At any time, about 50% of the Earth's skies are obscured by clouds. So they are almost always there and you just have to step outside and look up at the sky. Sailors and farmers have always used clouds as weather forecasters, and with a little practice the clouds can tell you a great deal about air conditions and the weather that may be coming (see **Fronts**).

Clouds are made up of microscopic water droplets, or at higher, colder levels, of minute ice crystals. They occur when the water vapor in the air condenses or freezes as air cools. In high-level clouds, which are forming at temperatures of around −40°F, the water is immediately frozen into tiny ice crystals. Although the temperature in even quite low-level clouds can be below 32°F, the water droplets are so small that they can be cooled far below normal freezing point without turning into ice (supercooling).

The water droplets formed by condensation in clouds are mostly no more than $\frac{1}{500}$ inch in diameter and can be much smaller. They are very light and remain suspended in the air or fall so slowly that they evaporate before they reach the ground. To fall as rain, droplets must be larger than $\frac{1}{250}$ inch, at which size they might fall as **drizzle** from very low clouds. True raindrops are much larger – around $\frac{1}{25}$ inch in diameter and hundreds of thousands of times heavier than cloud droplets. Raindrops are formed inside clouds in various complicated ways (see **Rain**) and only some clouds give rain.

Clouds form in many different situations. Small puffy clouds are generated on the top of up-currents of warm air that are rising above patches of ground heated by the sun. Clouds regularly form over mountains as air is forced to rise up the windward slope, cooling as it rises (see diagram below). **Fronts** and **cyclones** (depressions) are accompanied by extensive clouds as sheets of warm air are lifted high above a surface layer of cold air. **Mist** and **fog** are simply clouds that have formed close to the ground.

cool, moist air

warm, dry air

☁ CLOUD COVER

Clouds always cover about 50% of the Earth. Satellite pictures of the Earth from space show the belt of clouds over equatorial regions, where very warm moist air is continually rising and cooling. To either side of the Equator the air is clearer over deserts and dry grasslands. Whirlpools of clouds indicate **cyclones** (depressions). As well as holding vast amounts of water, which will eventually return to Earth as **rain** or **snow**, clouds help to regulate the temperature. In clear air with no clouds to reflect incoming sunlight, the surface temperature rises rapidly from a minimum just before dawn to a maximum around mid-afternoon. After that, outgoing radiation exceeds incoming and the surface starts to cool down. On a clear night, with no clouds to absorb and re-radiate heat, the surface continues to lose heat into space and rapidly cools. This is why desert nights are so cold after the baking heat of the day. At the other extreme, an overcast sky can reflect up to 80% of incoming sunlight. But although daytime is cooler, the clouds also prevent heat being lost, so there is less difference between day and night temperatures in cloudy conditions.

CLOUD FORMATION

CUMULUS CLOUD

sinking air

SUNLIGHT

bubble of warm air expands and cools

warm ground

Clouds are formed when air is cooled past its saturation point (see **Humidity**). Air is cooled adiabatically when it rises and is subject to lower **atmospheric pressure**. It rises on being heated by the ground (as in the diagram above), or when it is forced over an obstacle such as a mountain range or a layer of colder air. Small cumulus clouds typical of a fine day are formed when local heating causes a column of warm air (a thermal) to rise up through the colder surrounding air. The rising air expands as the pressure decreases. Air cools as it expands and so the rising air cools. Cold air can hold less water as vapor than can warm air. If warm moist air is cooled, therefore, it will eventually reach saturation, the point at which it is holding as much water vapor as it can at that temperature. If it is cooled further, water vapor starts to condense as droplets of liquid water, which become visible as cloud. In practice, clouds form before air reaches its saturation point as even the cleanest atmosphere contains particles of dust and salt which provide surfaces on which water condenses more easily.

There are two main types of cloud formation. **Cumulus** (or heap) **clouds** are produced by convection: "bubbles" of air are warmed at the surface and rise rapidly in an unstable atmosphere that tends to encourage upward air movement. **Layer** (or **stratus**) clouds are formed when more extensive sheets of moist air are lifted and cooled in a stable stratified atmosphere that tends to prevent upward air movement. Layer clouds form thick or thin sheets, or are broken by wind into billows, ridges, and rolls. Convection currents within a sheet of clouds give formations intermediate between cumulus and layer clouds. The main cloud types were first given their present names by meteorologists in the early 19th century. **Cirrus** (**1**), **cirrocumulus** (**2**), and **cirrostratus** (**3**) are high-level clouds made of ice crystals; **altocumulus** (**4**) and **altostratus** (**5**) are mid-level clouds; **stratocumulus** (**6**) and **stratus** (**7**) are low-level clouds. **Cumulus** clouds range from puffs of fleecy white (**8**) to towering dark thunderclouds, caled **cumulonimbus** (**9**), which reach right up to the top of the troposphere. **Nimbostratus** (**10**) clouds are dark low-based rainclouds.

The "mare's-tails" of the highest reaches of the sky are formed at around 25,000 feet and above, and are composed entirely of ice crystals. They may either take the form of small patches of white, silky cloud or be teased out by the winds of the upper atmosphere into fine strands with curled ends. When they stream out spectacularly over the sky they are often the first sign of a storm or an approaching warm front. The warm air borne high aloft above the cold resident air starts to condense and freezes instantaneously. The curls and hooks of cirrus are caused as fine trails of ice crystals fall slowly downwards. Ice clouds such as cirrus, **cirrostratus** and **cirrocumulus** form when air reaches its condensation point in temperatures below −40°F and immediately freezes. Ice clouds tend to grow rather than evaporate after freezing and can be long-lived.

CIRROCUMULUS (Cc)

The "mackerel sky" of the amateur weather forecaster, cirrocumulus is a high-level cloud forming at between 20,000 and 25,000 feet. It is composed of ice crystals, and develops a regular pattern of bands and rows of tiny white tufts of cloud that looks like mackerel skin. The old rhyme "mackerel sky; never long wet and never long dry" probably arose from observing that cirrocumulus sometimes precedes a storm or an approaching front bringing unsettled weather.

CIRROSTRATUS (Cs)

Cirrostratus is a transparent veil of ice crystal cloud forming between 20,000 and 25,000 feet. It often follows **cirrus** at the approach of a **warm front**, but is difficult to distinguish from haze caused by pollution. However, unlike haze, which is produced by particles of pollutants or by water droplets, the tiny ice crystals of which the cirrostratus veil is composed refract light, characteristically producing halos around the sun or the moon.

White or grayish clouds of the middle layers of the troposphere with their base at 7000 to 20,000 feet, altocumulus form higher than **stratocumulus** clouds and can originate from the higher reaches of stratocumulus or large cumulus clouds. They can also appear out of a cloudless sky as air is lifted near an approaching front. Altocumulus clouds are mainly composed of water droplets but may also contain ice crystals in their upper layers. They can take on many forms depending on the movement of the air, including parallel bands and cellular patterns. They often closely resemble stratocumulus clouds, and can be difficult to distinguish, but the individual cloud elements usually seem smaller as they are higher and farther away.

Altostratus is the smooth grayish or bluish layer of sometimes streaky clouds that covers all or part of the sky with a base between 7000 and 10,000 feet altitude. It is sometimes thin enough for the position of the sun to be seen through it, but not the clear outline. It consists mainly of supercooled water droplets, but ice crystals may form as a result of seeding by crystals falling from higher clouds. It replaces **cirrostratus** as a warm front approaches. If it thickens downwards in cold moist air it can form **nimbostratus**, the rainclouds producing persistent rain or snow.

Nimbostratus is a sheet of thick dark gray clouds, with a base between 3000 and 10,000 feet, which brings rain or snow depending on the air temperature beneath it. Nimbostratus clouds give a lowering wet gray sky of often persistent rain with detached patches of ragged gray clouds scudding along under the main cloud layer, or the almost black sky that heralds snow. They form when a sheet of warm moist air is forced upwards over cold air or over mountains, and when the resulting clouds can thicken enough to produce ice crystals in the upper layers. Nimbostratus clouds typically accompany **warm fronts** separating two moist air masses. In those conditions, **altostratus** clouds form first, thickening downwards in the cold wet air.

STRATOCUMULUS (Sc)

Stratocumulus is a common low-level cloud type, often formed when wind causes turbulence in moist air near the ground, mixing the air vertically and carrying moister air from the surface upwards. Stratocumulus is not a uniform grayish sheet like **stratus** (hence the addition of "cumulus" to the name), but is composed of more-or-less continuous white or grayish clumps, often arranged in bands or rolls, sometimes separated by clear sky. If the clouds are thicker they appear as light and dark patches. The cloud base ranges from around 1300 to 6500 feet and this cloud is composed of water droplets. It is quite common in winter when moist, warm air is moving northward. Stratocumulus is not very thick and tends to give only light drizzle (at temperatures above freezing), or light but sometimes persistent snow over hills or in sub zero temperatures. It can form when **cumulus** clouds hit a stable warm layer and the tops flatten out. The cumulus bases disperse, leaving a layer of stratocumulus. Stratocumulus can thicken downwards when surface air becomes moister, leaving the air above it clear and dry, as one often finds when climbing from clouds in the valley to sunshine higher up.

The featureless low sheet of gray clouds known generally as stratus has a base at around 1300 feet or lower. It forms in stable air conditions, but where wind at surface level keeps a layer of air below the cloud base well-mixed and too warm for condensation to occur. **Fog** is stratus clouds that have formed at ground level in the absence of turbulence, and conversely, fog lifted off the ground as conditions change becomes stratus. Stratus clouds are rarely thick enough to give rain, but can produce a light **drizzle**, or snow over higher ground. When the sun can be seen through them the outline is clear. Stratus can also form under a true raincloud (**nimbostratus**) when cold rain falls into a warmer layer, evaporating and making the layer moister and colder. It is often seen as ragged clouds (**scud**) blown along by the wind under the base of the raincloud.

The ragged scraps of **stratus** clouds that rise from a valley floor or run along near to the ground under large rainclouds are known as scud or fractus. They form and disperse rapidly. Under a raincloud, scud is formed in patches of lifted and cooled air that become moistened to saturation by the falling rain.

Cumulus clouds are common on sunny days when the ground is strongly heated by the sun. Fleets of these clouds often form, their bases all at the same level (see also **Cloud Streets**). Local heating of the ground produces up-currents of warm air (thermals). Each forms a cauliflower-shaped cloud as the air cools on rising and water vapor condenses. Cumulus clouds have a sharp outline caused by continuous formation of tiny droplets within the clouds, fed by its up-current of warm air, and rapid evaporation at the edges in the drier surrounding air. Small cumulus clouds last only about 15 to 20 minutes, evaporating as they drift away from the source of the warm air that feeds them. Cumulus clouds typically start to form in mid-morning as the ground warms up, are most extensive in mid-afternoon and disperse as the ground cools down. The cloud base is usually around 2300 feet, but may be as low as 1600 feet or as high as 6500 feet. The height of the cloud top is determined by the height at which the rising air has cooled to the temperature of the surrounding air and is no longer buoyant. Cumulus clouds are separated by descending air that compensates for the up-currents.

Over open country **cumulus** clouds often line up in a row,
which is called a cloud street. These formations are sometimes
the result of a succession of clouds being generated in the moist
air carried upwards by a thermal and then moving downwind.
On a sunny day over a flat uniform surface, regular parallel
streets of clouds may be formed, extending into the distance as
far as the eye can see. These are the result of the pattern of
updrafts and downdrafts created by general heating of the land
and the direction of the breeze. On satellite photographs large
areas of cloud streets are often spotted over the seas.

Small fair-weather **cumulus** can develop into much larger
cumulus clouds – known as cumulus congestus. They are among
the most fascinating clouds to watch as the persistent up-currents
of air within the cloud produce continually changing bubbles
and puffs on the upper surface. They develop in conditions
where the air inside the cloud remains warmer than the
surrounding air and so the cloud remains lighter than its
surroundings and continues to grow upwards, fed by the strong
up-currents of air within it. These rise at speeds of up to 65 feet
per second. Cumulus congestus tops can reach a height of
between 9000 and 16,500 feet. They sometimes flatten when
they meet a stable warm layer of air, but unlike a fully developed
cumulonimbus cloud, into which they can develop, this top is
not frozen. In midlatitude climates cumulus congestus clouds
rarely give rain but can give light showers. In the tropics,
however, large cumulus clouds developing from very moist air
are the source of heavy rain (see **Warm Rain**).

If you watch large **cumulus congestus** clouds rising you may be lucky enough to catch sight of the elusive pileus cloud. A small thin cloud with a smooth domed upper surface, it forms transitorily above rising cumulus. When cumulus is rising towards a horizontally moving air layer above it, the rising air ahead of it makes a small dent in the layer before it penetrates it. If the air is sufficiently moist a small cloud forms as air flows up and into the crest of this dent. Soon the cumulus top catches up with it and after draping the top for a few minutes, the pileus cloud disappears into the mass of rising clouds.

In extremely unstable atmospheric conditions huge dense cumulus clouds form, white at the edges but very dark at the base and towering the whole height of the troposphere. They grow from large cumulus clouds with bases between 1600 feet and 6600 feet, and tops at between 10,000 feet and 20,000 feet. In the unstable conditions, the air within these clouds is warmer than the surrounding air and so the clouds continue to grow, with very strong convectional up-currents within them. Heat produced as the massive amounts of water vapor condense helps feed the updrafts of warm air. The top of the clouds freezes to ice crystals, which grow steadily as water droplets are swept upwards and stick to them. The bubbling dome characteristic of growing cumulus becomes flattened once it freezes and often spreads out in a wide plume (the anvil) on the prevailing high-level winds. Fully developed cumulonimbus clouds are thunderclouds, which bring heavy **rain** or **hail** showers and **thunderstorms**.

MAMMA

The underside of the spreading anvil of a **cumulonimbus** stormcloud is sometimes a mass of rounded hanging pouches of falling ice crystals that are revealed when low sun strikes the undersurface of the anvil. The pouches appear on the cloud after or towards the end of the storm and are called mamma from their obvious resemblance to breasts. They can also appear on the base of the raincloud as falling small droplets cluster together.

In the evening after a warm sunny day, tall thin cumulus "towers" can sometimes be seen sprouting from a thin **altocumulus** cloud layer forming over low hills, a valley or a narrow stretch of water. If the towers are ascending into dry air they quickly evaporate into fleecy "floccus." Thin towers can sometimes also be seen sprouting from the top and sides of large cumulus clouds. They each represent an up-current of warm air. Altocumulus castellanus indicates unstable air and thus sometimes precedes heat-generated thunderstorms.

Clouds of all sorts are especially frequent in the mountains. The uneven and varied land surface and high altitudes create excellent conditions for the formation of both convective (**cumulus**) clouds and layer clouds (see **Clouds**). Mountains also have some cloud formations typically their own. The clouds that often hang almost permanently over some mountains, especially those near the sea, are caused by the uplift and cooling of moist air when it meets the windward slope. Clouds form on the higher windward slopes, often also shedding their moisture as rain or snow. Once over the summit the air starts to descend. It is compressed by the increasing pressure and starts to warm up. Having shed most of its moisture it is usually also drier by this time and so the cloud cap does not extend far below the summit on the leeward side. Although a cloud cap seems stationary, it is not the same cloud all the time but is continually being formed in the airflow. Clouds formed by forced lifting of air over an obstacle such as a mountain range are known as orographic clouds.

A lens-shaped (lenticular) cloud can form high above a mountain
when a stream of high-level moist air rises as it flows over the
summit. If there are several layers of moist air, piles of lenticular
clouds are formed looking uncannily like "flying saucers," as in
this illustration of lenticular clouds in Antarctica. A less spectacular
series of lenticular clouds is formed when a stable airflow forced
up a mountain slope forms waves after it clears the summit, the so-
called "lee waves," The descending air is carried along on these
waves and cooled as it rises to the crests. If it is cooled to saturation,
a train of shallow lenticular clouds, steadily decreasing in size,
can form to leeward of the mountain.

High isolated peaks do not present enough surface area to the wind to force it to flow over the summit. The airstream divides below the summit and the turbulence caused makes the air rise slightly to leeward of the mountain. With a moist airstream this rise is sufficient to form a cloud which streams out with the wind and gradually evaporates from the base to form a roughly triangular or banner shape.

Contrails (an abbreviation of condensation trails) are the straight lines of clouds that form in the wake of an aircraft. They are produced by condensation of the water vapor emitted from the aircraft's engines (water vapor being a product of fuel combustion). In dry air they disperse quickly but in moist air they persist for a long time, gradually thinning out and becoming less distinct. The space between the engines and the start of the contrail is a result of the air coming from the engines being too hot to condense immediately. Distrails (dissipation trails) are paths of clean air evaporated from a cloud by the heat of the engines as an aircraft passes through it.

FOG and MIST

Fog and mist are in many respects simply clouds that form immediately above the ground and, like clouds, they occur for different reasons in different situations. In all cases a layer of air next to the surface must cool below its condensation point to remain suspended in the air. Fog and mist drops are very small. Fog drops are similar in size to those in clouds, around $\frac{1}{500}$ inch in diameter; mist drops are even smaller, less than $\frac{1}{25,000}$ inch across. Fog and mist form when the air is fairly calm, but not usually absolutely still. In meteorological terms fog is any atmospheric condition that obscures surface visibility to less than 3000 feet; highway accidents and airport disruptions are usually caused by thick fog – visibility worse than 600 feet. Mist is thinner, reducing visibility to between two-thirds of a mile and $1\frac{1}{4}$ miles. A similar condition due to dust or smoke in the atmosphere is called haze. When moist air close to the ground is cooled in completely still air, **dew** often forms. When the air and ground cool to below 32° F, **frost** is likely, as the moisture in the air freezes out as ice crystals.

☁ RADIATION FOG

Fog that forms in river valleys and damp hollows and over low-lying land at night is produced when still moist air is chilled as the ground under it loses heat during the night. It is therefore the result of radiational cooling, from which it gets its name. Radiation fog only develops over land and is most common when nights are long – in autumn and winter – when it can last all through the following day and even not lift for days. In summer the sun is generally warm enough to shift it early in the morning. A clear sky, so that the ground cools right down at night, and only a very slight movement of the air (around 3 to 10 feet per second) are needed to produce it. If the air is completely still, however, only a very thin layer of fog forms at ground level; too much wind and the fog is lifted to form low **stratus** cloud. Radiation fog is often patchy, depending for its formation on the contours of the land and whether the land surface loses heat readily. It tends to gather in hollows and valleys because air becomes denser and heavier as it cools and runs down to the bottom of a slope. A layer of radiation fog can be up to 900 feet deep, but is usually less.

Fog at sea is usually the result of warm moist air moving slowly over a cold surface. The air cools and water vapor condenses. Fog produced in this way is called advection fog to distinguish it from **radiation fog**. It is common at sea when warm moist air moves over a cold current, or when warm tropical air moves in over colder waters. The regular fog off the coast of California is the result of warm moist air from the Pacific rolling in over the cold ocean current (the California Current). Advection fog is very similar to **stratus** cloud, but is produced when the air is calmer close to the ground. The air immediately above the surface remains cold and the "cloud" stays as a layer on the ground. Wind speeds of about 15 feet per second are ideal conditions for advection fog and it generally makes a layer around 300 feet thick. Fog coming in from the sea often clears when it reaches the warmer land surface. When advection fog forms over land it tends to disperse during the day as the land warms up, and reforms at night. Daytime warming or increased wind speeds can also lift the fog off the ground to produce stratus cloud. Hill fogs are sometimes caused this way.

STEAM FOG

Steam fog or "Arctic smoke" is the result of cold air moving over warm water. For steam fog to form there has to be a large temperature difference (at least 18°F) between water and air. Evaporation from the warmer water into the already cold air saturates it almost immediately and the vapor condenses. This type of fog is often seen in the Arctic when cold air from above ice and snow blows over relatively warm water and the surface appears to steam. It rarely forms a layer more than about 50 feet thick and is often much thinner. A similar phenomenon is seen over sun-warmed roads in summer after a sudden shower, and when cold air moves over the warmer water of lakes and rivers.

Smog is a combination of smoke or other pollutants and fog. Now that the "London" smogs caused by smoke and sulphur dioxide from domestic coal fires are a thing of the past, the worst pollution threat to human health and comfort in cities comes from the exhaust fumes of motor vehicles. Exhaust emissions contain carbon monoxide, oxides of nitrogen, various hydrocarbons, lead (from leaded gasoline), and small amounts of sulfur dioxide (SO_2) as well as carbon dioxide (CO_2). In hot sunny conditions the effects of exhaust pollution are made worse by the formation of "photochemical smog." Sunlight acts on nitric oxides to form ozone and nitrogen dioxide. Together with formaldehyde and peroxyacetyl nitrate (PAN), these gases irritate eyes and lungs and also damage plants. Visibility is reduced as the increased number of particles in the air create haze and act as nuclei on which moisture condenses into fog and mist. The photochemical smogs of Los Angeles persist for days as the polluted air is trapped under an upper warm layer (an inversion). Cars in California have to be fitted by law with catalytic converters to reduce emissions of some pollutants.

☁ DEW

The tiny droplets of dew that bejewel cobwebs and leaves on a still morning in the fall are formed when the ground loses heat at night, cooling the air immediately in contact with the ground down to the dew point. At this point water vapor in the air condenses onto any cold surface, just as a glass of cold water will cool the surrounding air enough to form condensation on the outside. A clear night and still air are ideal conditions for a dewy morning. Dew on grass is sometimes confused with drops of water produced by the plants themselves (in the physiological process known as guttation) and that cannot evaporate into the surrounding water-saturated air. Guttation drops are large drops usually hanging at the tip of the leaf, whereas the smaller dewdrops cover the flat surface. The heaviest dews occur when moist warm air moves in over surfaces that are already very cold, as sometimes happens when the weather suddenly changes after a cold spell. In places with adequate rainfall, dew provides a very small proportion of water returning to the ground, but it can be an essential source of moisture for plant and animal life in dry or desert areas where there is little rainfall.

Frost is likely to form when air and ground are colder than 32°F.
When air that is being cooled in contact with cold ground
reaches its saturation point at sub-zero temperatures, the water
vapor in the air freezes to form needle like crystals of ice which
are deposited on the ground as a sparkling white layer of hoar
frost. Hoar frost is most common after a clear calm cold night.
The delicate tracings of fern frost that form on the insides of
window panes in very cold weather are the result of
crystallization of supercooled water drops. The first ice crystals
trigger off a chain reaction to make the feather-like patterns. A
"black frost" (when air temperature is less than 32°F) can occur
without visible signs of hoar frost when air is very dry and is not
saturated at sub-zero temperature. It is very damaging to plants.
Another dangerous manifestation of frost is rime. This is a
covering of ice that builds up on surfaces when they are exposed
to supercooled fog (fog in which the water droplets are colder
than 32°F but have not frozen). On contact with a surface,
supercooled fog freezes and crusts of ice may build up. Icing on
aircraft is due to this phenomenon.

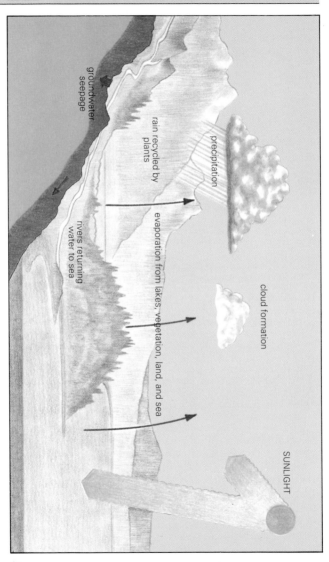

groundwater
seepage

rain recycled by
plants

precipitation

rivers returning
water to sea

evaporation from lakes, vegetation, land, and sea

cloud formation

SUNLIGHT

The Water Cycle

Although rain and its winter equivalent, snow, are sometimes unwelcome, they are essential to life. They replenish the moisture in the ground and fill the lakes and rivers that we depend on for water. Precipitation, the meteorological term for water fall-out in all its forms, is the final turn in the cycle that starts when water is evaporated from oceans, lakes, the ground, and vegetation by the Sun's energy. Clouds form when the moist air is forced to rise and cool. But not all clouds produce rain or snow. Rain clouds occur along the cold and warm **fronts** in **cyclones**, where a layer of warmer air rises above cold air, cooling and condensing as it ascends. Local showers and storms are produced from large **cumulonimbus** clouds, which arise by convection. Rain clouds are also formed when moist air is forced to rise as it meets high ground (orographic clouds). As illustrated opposite, moisture-laden air from over the oceans moves in over the coast. Meeting high ground, it rises and the water vapor within it condenses into clouds. In the right conditions the clouds become thick enough to produce rain (or snow if the temperature is cold enough). Because most of the rain tends to fall on the coastal slopes and summits, the landward slopes of coastal mountain ranges are usually much drier. Continental interiors in mid-latitudes, away from the equatorial rain forest belts, are also drier than coastal regions.

Rainfall statistics gathered throughout the year at one location give the "point rainfall" for that site. Two of the wettest places in the world are Mt. Wai-'ale-'ale on the Hawaiian island of Kauai, with an average rainfall of over 400 inches of rain per year, and Cherrapungi, in the mountains of Assam, India, where an (exceptional) annual rainfall of over 1000 inches has been recorded, almost all of it in the monsoon season in late spring and summer. In contrast, average annual rainfall in the USA ranges from around 2 inches in the southwest to almost 150 inches in the Cascade Mountains of Washington and Oregon.

Water is stored in natural reservoirs – in rocks, soil, lakes, rivers, and oceans. The absence of rain or snow that would normally fall is a **drought**, which can occur at any time of the year and in any climate. In contrast, more rain than the terrain is adapted to causes **flooding**.

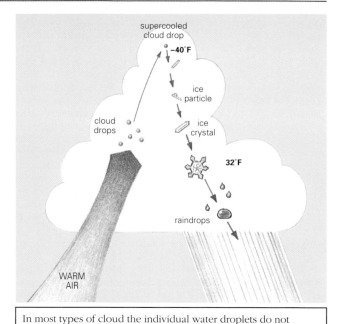

supercooled
cloud drop

−40°F

ice
particle

cloud
drops

ice
crystal

32°F

raindrops

WARM
AIR

In most types of cloud the individual water droplets do not
survive long enough to form drops large and heavy enough to
reach the ground before evaporating. Rain falling from
nimbostratus or **cumulonimbus** clouds has in fact started its
journey as snowflakes originating high in the frozen cloud top.
There cloud drops freeze into tiny ice crystals. They collide with
and freeze the small supercooled cloud drops and grow into
snowflakes. Once they have grown heavy enough the
snowflakes start falling, melting as they pass through the warmer
layers of the cloud. These droplets are large enough to keep
falling and collide with and gather smaller cloud drops to them.
Drops that reach a size of $\frac{1}{25}$ inch or more by the time they reach
the base of the cloud fall as rain. Because of their resistance to
the air, falling raindrops are not tear-shaped, as pictured in
cartoons, but resemble small buns. The largest raindrops are
around $\frac{1}{4}$ inch in diameter and fall at a speed of 26 feet per
second. The occasional very large raindrops are likely to be
hailstones or snowflakes that have melted just before reaching
the ground.

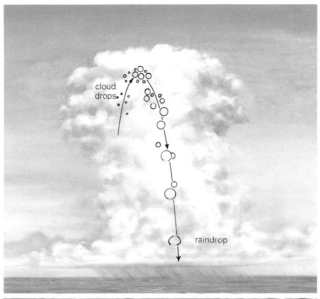

cloud drops

raindrop

In the tropics, rain falls from clouds whose tops remain unfrozen. Updrafts in large, moist tropical clouds are slow but steady; cloud droplets remain in the cloud long enough (30 to 40 minutes) to grow large and coalesce with other drops to form raindrops. Rain produced in this way is often called "warm" rain to distinguish it from rain originating from ice crystals. Even outside the tropics, warm rain sometimes falls from large **cumulus** clouds in evening, as the cooling air slows down convection. This is the usual explanation of evening showers that appear after a fine day of cumulus clouds but no rain. Cumulus clouds forming over the sea can also give warm rain, as upward convection currents over water are weaker than over land, so that cloud droplets are not swept out of the cloud to evaporate but have time to grow.

ACID RAIN

$$SO_2 + H_2O \rightarrow H_2SO_4 + H_2SO_3$$

sulfuric acid   sulfurous acid

SO_2

ACID RAIN

Sulfur dioxide (SO_2) released by the burning of fossil fuels
(particularly oil and coal) becomes transformed in the air and in
clouds into sulfurous and sulfuric acids. Harmful to animals and
plants, they can be carried long distances and are eventually
washed out in rain. Acid rain gradually acidifies lakes, rivers, and
soils on which it falls. The effects of acid rain on the environment
first came to notice in western and southern Scandinavia and in
Canada where lakes had become acid and lifeless. Acid rain has
also been blamed for the widespread damage to forests in central
Europe. Sulfur dioxide also contributed in the past to the
choking "London fogs" (see **Smog**), which claimed thousands of
lives. The use of smokeless fuels has made the air of our cities
much cleaner in this respect, and there are stricter controls on
the amount of sulfur dioxide that can be emitted from power
plants and factories. Acid in the air in cities (in this case mainly
from nitrous oxides in car exhausts) is also responsible for
damage to limestone and marble buildings, such as the ancient
Parthenon in Athens, Greece.

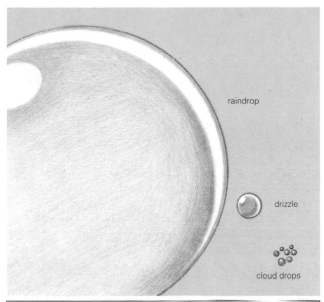

raindrop

drizzle

cloud drops

Low, thin clouds that cannot give rain can sometimes give a fine drizzle. Drizzle drops are small ($\frac{1}{250}$ to $\frac{1}{50}$ inch in diameter) and drizzle is quite distinct from light rain, where the drops are proper raindrops, $\frac{1}{25}$ inch or more across. Drizzle falls only from very low clouds. This is because a water droplet $\frac{1}{250}$ inch across can fall only 300 feet or so through clear air before it evaporates. In contrast, a raindrop of $\frac{1}{25}$ inch across can fall 3000 feet before evaporating. Drizzle usually falls through cool moist air, which slows evaporation. Neither rain nor drizzle can fall from thin clouds composed only of very small drops, and they cannot fall from high-based clouds because the falling drops or crystals simply evaporate before reaching the ground. Trails of ice crystals (virga) are sometimes seen falling from high clouds and disappearing before they reach the ground.

Rainfall is considered light when it falls at a rate of less than
$\frac{1}{50}$ inch per hour, moderate at $\frac{1}{50}$ to $\frac{1}{6}$ inch per hour and heavy at
over $\frac{1}{6}$ inch per hour. Showers are short bursts of rain, often
heavy but generally soon over. They usually fall from large
cumulonimbus clouds. These occur at and behind cold fronts,
which therefore bring showery weather rather than persistent
rain. Large cumulus clouds can hold an enormous amount of
water, which empties over the land suddenly and with great
force. Isolated thunderclouds can give heavy showers of such
intensity that they cause local flooding. Some exceptional
cloudbursts have been recorded: in Montana, over 12 inches of
rain fell in 42 minutes; in Hampstead in London, UK, 7 inches of
rain in 2½ hours caused flash floods. Showers usually mean that a
cloud is nearing the end of its life, as the warm updrafts that feed
it are overwhelmed by the downward rush of cold air and rain.
Light showers can fall from quite small cumulus clouds,
especially those that develop over the sea where convection
currents are weak (see **Warm Rain**).

Floods occur for many reasons. On low-lying coasts, the greatest danger is from **storm surges** accompanying hurricanes or depressions, and made greater by high winds and high tides. Inland, natural and man-made water courses and reservoirs are adapted to cope with the average rainfall and become overloaded if too much falls in a short space of time. The floods in Florence, Italy in early November 1966, in which many art treasures were lost or damaged, were caused by the River Arno overflowing its banks after a day of continuous rain following an unusually wet October that had already filled the river almost brimful. Less severe flash floods often occur in towns and cities when sudden localized cloudbursts overload drains, which become blocked with debris. The effects of heavy rain in mountain regions are often made worse by landslides and mudslides, especially if the area is naturally dry and treeless or where deforestation or development have removed the protective cover of vegetation that would normally soak up the water. Flooding can also occur if the soil, which normally absorbs large amounts of water, is baked hard by drought or frozen solid in winter.

DROUGHT

In meteorological terms, drought is an absence of the rain that would normally fall and so the definition of a drought will vary from place to place. A drought in regions where rain is expected all the year round, as in parts of the eastern United States, might be a period of only 15 or more consecutive days without rain (or with less than $\frac{1}{12}$ inch per day). Tucson, Arizona, in contrast, regularly experiences more than 70 consecutive days without rain in the dry spring months. Droughts have many different causes. In California, they can be due to changes in the offshore current which lead to cooling of the sea surface. This means that the air coming in from the Pacific is less moist. The droughts in the Great Plains in the 1950s were caused by persistent areas of high pressure that deflected rain-bearing depressions northwards. Severe drought is a regular occurrence in parts of the world and contributes to the continuing famines in Africa. The lands around the Sahara, where life depends on a seasonal rainfall of 10 to 20 inches, have had several cycles of rainless years.

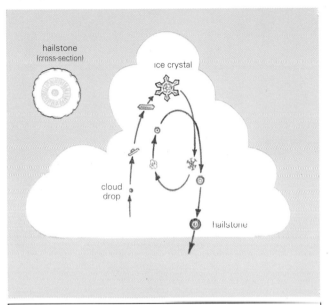

hailstone
(cross-section)

ice crystal

cloud
drop

hailstone

Thunderclouds (**cumulonimbus**) sometimes produce hail and not rain, even in summer. Hailstones are more or less round hard pellets of ice, and in cross-section layers of clear and opaque ice can often be seen. Hailstones are formed as ice crystals are repeatedly tossed up and down in the cloud by violent air currents. They coalesce with supercooled cloud drops, which freeze to form layers of ice around the original nucleus. Clear ice forms when the hailstone is in the lower, warmer, part of the cloud, where water freezes fairly slowly; the opaque layers are acquired nearer the top of the cloud where the drops freeze instantaneously on contact. Hailstones are usually ⅛ inch to 2 inches in diameter but larger stones, up to 8 inches across, have fallen. Severe hailstorms are commonest over the plains in continental interiors, where large active thunderclouds are common. Soft pellets of ice (known as "graupel") are snow that has melted and partly refrozen. They consist of a soft core surrounded by a thin layer of ice. Small insects and even frogs have formed the nucleus of hailstones, having been swept up into the clouds by strong up-currents.

The snow that transforms even the dreariest landscape starts high in the frozen tops of large thick clouds. Minute ice crystals form in the very low temperatures there (below $-40°$ F) and crystallize more vapor around them to build beautifully symmetrical "snowflakes." When these become heavy enough they start to fall. If the temperature from the top of the cloud all the way down to the ground is below $32°$ F, the snowflakes reach the ground intact, growing larger on their way down. Snow falls even in the tropics, but only over high mountains. Dry powdery snow falls when temperatures are so low that the falling crystals do not melt and refreeze when they touch and so do not form large soft flakes. Dry snow is very light and extremely penetrating but is ideal for skiing. Wet snow, in contrast, is composed of crystals that have melted and refrozen together to form soft flakes. It makes good snowballs and snowmen as it sticks together easily. Wet snow falls more commonly in maritime regions and dry snow over continental interiors. Some 36 inches depth of dry snow, compared with 7 inches of wet snow, have a water content equal to 1 inch of rain.

Ice crystals and "snowflakes" come in a variety of forms, including needles, hexagons, columns, prisms, and six-pointed stars. The shape depends on the temperature of the air through which they fall. They all have a six-sided symmetry however, which stems from the molecular structure of frozen water. Snowflakes are formed of many of these microscopic hexagonal crystals frozen together. The star-shaped crystals popularly called "snowflakes" are known technically as dendritic crystals. They are formed in fairly moist air at temperatures around 5°F. No two crystals are identical and the individual shapes are the result of the growth of the crystal through a complicated sequence of evaporation, condensation, sublimation (direct conversion of water vapor to ice), and deposition around a tiny hexagonal ice nucleus.

A snowstorm technically becomes a blizzard in strong winds (30 mph or more). The snow drives horizontally, piling up in huge drifts when it comes up against an obstacle. This means that the same amount of snowfall in blizzard conditions usually creates many more problems than when it forms an even cover. Deep lanes are filled to the top, leaving neighboring fields swept bare, and drifts of hard, wind-packed snow block city streets. Blizzards may also be caused by strong winds whipping up already fallen snow, as in the Arctic and Antarctic. In more temperate regions, the source of air for a blizzard is originally moist and fairly warm, as very cold air cannot hold enough moisture to produce heavy persistent snow. The combination of cold and wind in a blizzard is very dangerous to human beings, as a phenomenon known as the wind chill factor causes air temperatures to drop. Properly clothed, a person is safe in air temperatures down to around −18°F if it is calm. But if a wind of 30 mph is blowing, the temperature experienced drops from −18°F to −76°F. There is then a danger of frostbite and of death from exposure, and bare flesh rapidly freezes.

When mild weather comes to snow-covered hills and mountains, melting loosens the snow on the slopes. Masses of snow break loose and slide downhill in an avalanche. A whole layer of snow can break away along a fault, or a rush of snow may fan out from a single point; overhanging cornices are also prone to break off. Avalanches often also occur on steep slopes in heavy snow storms as the slope cannot carry the extra weight of snow. Snow ready to move can be set off by wind, the movement of skiers or even by a sharp noise. Avalanches move fast, rapidly engulfing everything in their path. Snow can move at up to 50 mph along the ground and at higher speeds becomes airborne. Avalanches are particularly dangerous in heavily populated mountain areas and areas developed for winter sports.

Winds

Winds are the horizontal movement of air as it flows from an area of high pressure to an area of lower pressure. On the global scale, the air in the lower atmosphere is circulating continually as heat is redistributed from the equator to the poles (see **General Circulation**). As these great air movements sweep the surface of the globe, they become the reliable **Global Winds** that blow steadily over the oceans. At a more local level, winds are generated in many different ways. Air is twisted around **cyclones** (areas of low pressure) and **anticyclones** (areas of high pressure) (see **Coriolis Effect**), is forced up over mountains and funneled through valleys (see **Local Winds**). In cities and towns, tall buildings create their own local circulation. **Breezes** are often generated by localized heating and cooling of the air as the land warms up during the day and cools down at night. Absolutely windless days are rare in most places, and when they occur, are usually associated with the presence of a large area of stationary high pressure. In contrast, the autumn and winter **gales** and **storms** that hit the western coasts of Europe accompany deep depressions (cyclones) traveling in from the Atlantic. The strongest winds are generated in **hurricanes** and **tornadoes** (estimated at up to 400 mph), and in gusts on high mountains (up to 220 mph). Winds are described in terms of their speed and the direction from which they are blowing. A westerly wind, for example, blows from the west towards the east. The windiest place in the world is Eastern Adelie Land on the coast of Antarctica. Strong winds blow continuously down off the icecap towards the sea, reaching hurricane-force (more than 73 mph) on one day out of three.

Wind speeds are described in different ways in different countries: in meters per second, kilometers per hour, miles per hour, or knots (nautical miles* per hour) or a force number on the Beaufort Scale (see pages 124/125). The speed of the wind depends on the steepness of the pressure gradient that is creating it. The steeper the gradient the greater the wind speed. On the **weather map**, closely spaced isobars indicate a steep pressure gradient and a strong wind. Because of the Coriolis effect, winds blow along the isobars and not directly across them from high to low pressure as one might expect.

* 1 nautical mile = 1852 meters (2027 yards) or 1.15 statute miles

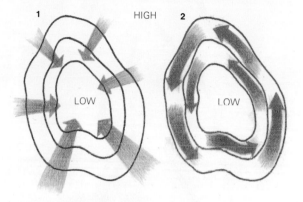

Air naturally flows from an area of high pressure to an area of lower pressure. Looking at the low pressure system illustrated here, we might therefore expect the wind to blow into the depression straight across the isobars (**1**). But instead, the wind blows round the center of the depression parallel to the isobars (**2**). This happens because the Earth's eastwards rotation deflects all horizontal air movement to the right in the Northern Hemisphere (and to the left in the Southern Hemisphere). This is the Coriolis effect. Winds therefore blow counterclockwise around **cyclones** (low pressure areas) and clockwise around **anticyclones** (high pressure areas) in the Northern Hemisphere and the other way round in the Southern. This gives us the rule (known as "Buys Ballot's Law") that if you stand with your back to the wind, the area of low pressure will always be on your left (in the Northern Hemisphere). A shift in the direction of the wind often means a change in the weather. A backing wind is one shifting in a counterclockwise direction and is a sign of low-pressure areas and approaching storms. Veering winds are shifting clockwise and are generally a sign of high pressure and fine weather.

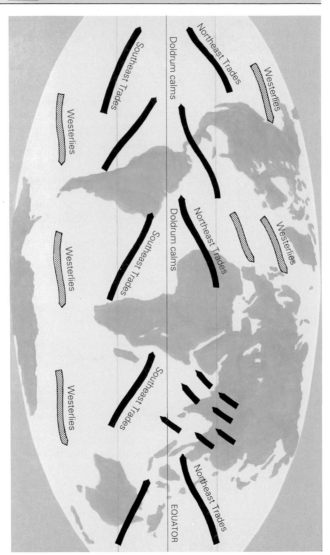

Global Winds

The pattern of surface winds is a reflection of the general circulation of the atmosphere and of the distribution of persistent areas of high and low pressure. The map shows the main winds that blow in winter. At the Equator are the doldrums, where winds rarely blow and where, in the days of sailing ships, vessels could become becalmed for weeks. Between 30° North and 30° South over the Atlantic and the Pacific are the belts of the Trade Winds, blowing steadily from the northeast in the Northern Hemisphere and the southeast in the Southern for most of the year. Around 30°N is a subtropical belt of high pressure with little surface wind (the so-called "Horse Latitudes" of the old sailing ships). To the north the polar westerlies blow strongly across the Pacific and the Atlantic in winter, and carry weather out of the Pacific onto the west coast of North America and out of the Atlantic to western Europe. A strong westerly wind blows around the southern Atlantic and Pacific Oceans all the year round, and these latitudes are often known as the "Roaring Forties."

In some parts of the world, changes in the location of high and low pressure centers from winter to summer result in a seasonal change of prevailing winds. The most famous of these are the monsoon winds of the Indian subcontinent. On the large map opposite you can see the situation in winter. Dry winds blow from the North, from the high pressure area over snow-covered northern Asia. In summer, as illustrated below, the area of high pressure collapses and moisture-laden winds, the monsoons, blow in from the south, bringing long-awaited rain to the Indian subcontinent.

✒ BREEZES

Breezes are winds of up to 31 mph (Force 1 to 6 on the Beaufort Scale; see pages 124/125). The strongest breezes (Force 6) set large branches swaying and blow umbrellas inside out. At sea they raise fair-sized waves with long white crests and some blowing spray. The illustration shows a Force 5 breeze (19 to 24 mph). A gentler breeze often blows from sea to shore, especially on tropical coasts, on a hot sunny day. This sea breeze reaches speeds of up to 12 mph (around Force 3) and is caused by the land warming up and cooling down more quickly than the sea. On a sunny day, air above land is rapidly warmed. The warm air rises, and cooler air from over the sea moves in at surface level to take its place. Sea breezes outside the tropics are strongest when the temperature difference between land and sea is greatest – in spring and early summer when the land is warming up but the sea is still cool. Daily warming and cooling also cause the typical reversal of wind direction in morning and evening in mountain valleys. The sides of the valley are warmed in daytime causing a warm wind to blow up the slope. At night, cold air flows down the sides of the valley.

Winds between 32 and 63 mph are gales (Force 7 to 10 on the Beaufort Scale, see pages 124/125) and winds above 64 mph are storm force winds (Force 11). The picture illustrates a Force 8 gale (39 to 46 mph), which blows whole trees about and tears off twigs and leaves. Above 72 mph winds officially become hurricane-force (Force 12) as such wind speeds are rarely maintained outside tropical cyclonic storms (**hurricanes**). True hurricanes are generated only over tropical waters. Gales and storm-force winds outside the tropics are almost always associated with depressions, and are often known as "frontal storms," as the depressions are generated along the **fronts** between warm and cold **air masses**. Gales and storms are regularly encountered at sea, but storm-force winds are seldom experienced inland.

Hurricanes are revolving systems of intensely low pressure, which form only over tropical seas and in which wind speeds often exceed 100 mph. A tropical storm is raised to hurricane status when steady winds exceed 73 mph. Wind speed increases towards the center, the "eye" of the hurricane, which is an area of relative calm around 7 miles across. Pressure in the center is typically around 950 mb but may be as low as 870 mb. The whole system measures 50 to 500 miles in diameter. Hurricanes form only over tropical waters as they require a continual source of very moist warm air. Officially called "tropical revolving storms," they are known as hurricanes in the Caribbean, typhoons in the China Sea, tropical cyclones in the Indian Ocean and "Willy-Willies" off Australia. Air is thrown outwards from the center to spiral upwards in a ring around the eye. A wall of towering **cumulonimbus** clouds up to 7 miles high surrounds the eye, giving torrential rain. As a hurricane passes over, an observer experiences a furious storm blowing from one direction followed by a calm period, after which the storm returns, blowing in the opposite direction.

A tornado or "twister" is an intense whirlwind, spinning down in a funnel from the base of a large thundercloud or hurricane and often accompanied by rain or hail and lightning. Tornadoes mainly arise during severe thunderstorms that occur along or in front of strong cold fronts. The tip of the funnel ranges from 50 to 100 feet diameter, and produces a swath of devastation along its path where it touches the ground. The updraft inside the tornado sucks up dust, debris, and even buildings. Wind speed in a tornado is difficult to measure but may reach around 400 mph. The path of a tornado is a few miles long on average, but they can travel erratically, with the funnel lifting off the ground at intervals. Tornadoes usually spin counterclockwise in the Northern Hemisphere. Devastating tornadoes occur most frequently on the central Plains of the United States from Texas to Kansas in late spring, with around 900 tornadoes each year. Tornadoes cause damage by the direct impact of the wind, magnified by its twisting, and also by the intensely low pressure in the center. As a tornado passes over, buildings explode outwards as the air inside them is sucked out.

Tornado-type whirlwinds occurring over the sea create waterspouts. The low pressure inside the spinning funnel sucks up water from the surface to join the funnel cloud. Waterspouts do not last very long (up to 20 minutes) and are not as violent as tornadoes. They are common off the coast of Florida and typically have diameters of 40 to 80 feet. Smaller and much less intense funnels of spinning air, invisible until they whirl debris up from the surface, often form over land surfaces that heat up rapidly. They usually last only a few minutes. Unlike tornadoes they are not formed by storm clouds but rise from the ground as warmed, rising air is set spinning by the wind. Small vortices occurring over water are called "water-devils," those over land "land-devils." "Dust-devils" and "sand-pillars" occur over dry dusty ground and over desert respectively.

STORM SURGES

Storm surges are exceptionally large waves, often called "tidal waves" although they are not primarily caused by tides. They are the result of the passage of a fast moving deep **depression**, and often accompany **hurricanes**. The rapid change of pressure creates a swell wave which grows as it travels across the sea and is channeled onto a coastline. Storm surges can raise sea level by up to 16 feet which, added to wind-whipped waves up to 30 feet high, causes extensive flooding on low-lying coasts. In 1900, Galveston, Texas was flooded by a storm surge during a hurricane and 5000 lives were lost. Today, on the eastern and southern US seaboard, advance warnings of storm surges mean that areas at risk can be evacuated. Storm surges caused by tropical cyclones periodically devastate the low-lying coastal regions of Bangladesh. Very large waves can also be raised by a combination of wind and tide, especially when the wind is blowing uninterrupted across a wide stretch of ocean. "Tidal" waves due to wind, tide, and pressure changes should not be confused with "tsunami," the large, fast-traveling waves (up to 200 feet high) caused by earthquakes.

LOCAL WINDS

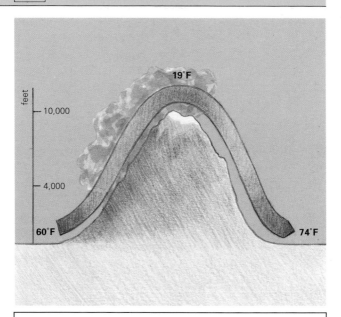

The lay of the land generates local and seasonal winds in many parts of the world. In North America, the strong dry and warm Chinook that sometimes blows down the eastern slopes of the Rocky Mountains is a föhn wind (so-called because this type of wind was first identified in the Swiss Alps). It occurs when air is forced to descend and becomes warmed adiabatically as it does so. This can happen when air is forced over the mountain range and loses its moisture on the upward journey (see illustration), or when stationary air over the summit forces air to descend rapidly from higher levels in the atmosphere. This wind is also called the "snow-eater," as it can raise the temperature at the foot of the eastern slope by 18 to 27°F in an hour and clear the slopes of snow in a single day. An exceptional rise of 49°F (from −4°F to 45°F) was recorded in 2 minutes at Spearfish, South Dakota on one January day in 1943. At other times, a strong cold wind blows down the eastern slopes of the Rocky Mountains, reaching up to 100 mph. On the Gulf coast of Texas, winds blow inland from the sea in summer, and a similar phenomenon occurs on the shores of the Great Lakes.

The sky appears blue because light from the Sun is scattered by
the molecules of the gases that make up the air and by tiny
particles in the atmosphere. The shortest wavelengths of light
– the blue end of the spectrum – are scattered most. Away from
the direct path of the sunlight we therefore see the sky as blue,
as we receive the scattered blue rays from all parts of the sky.
The shorter the path that sunlight has to travel through the lower
atmosphere and the cleaner the atmosphere, the bluer the sky, as
only the blue rays are scattered. Direct sunlight is yellow as the
longer (red) wavelengths in the beam reach us directly with little
scattering. But when the Sun is low in the sky, as at sunset, its
rays reach us through a greater thickness of atmosphere. By the
time the light reaches our eyes, all the shorter wavelengths have
been scattered out of the direct beam, and so the Sun appears
much redder and less bright. Scattering of the longer
wavelengths also colors the sky red and gold. Polluted skies
often look reddish and hazy as the increased number and size of
particles in the air scatter the longer wavelengths of light.

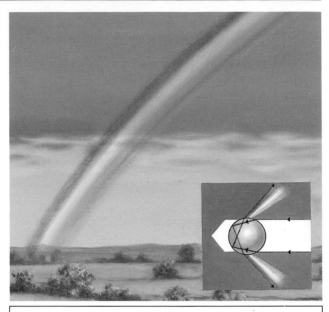

When the Sun comes out after a shower you may see a rainbow as the sunlight is refracted and reflected from millions of raindrops, separating the light rays into the colors of the spectrum. Light bends slightly as it enters a raindrop (refraction) and is then reflected back towards the viewer from the curved back wall of the droplet. So you only see a rainbow when you are standing between the Sun and the curtain of raindrops. Light of different wavelengths is bent at different angles and so the colors become clearly separated, with violet on the inside and red on the outside. Although each droplet refracts the whole spectrum of colors, the viewer sees violet rays from one set of raindrops, yellow from another, and so on, because of the different angles of refraction. The rainbow arc is part of a notional circle with the head of the viewer's shadow as the center. Each person sees his or her own unique rainbow and can never reach its end, as the rainbow moves with them as they look at the raindrops from a different angle. Two internal reflections within droplets create a duller secondary rainbow outside the first, with the order of the colors reversed.

BROCKENSPECTER

Mountaineers may sometimes see the magnified shadows of themselves or other objects projected onto a bank of cloud or fog below when the Sun is low in the sky behind them. The shadow is enlarged as it falls through a depth of water droplets. Although this strange phenomenon may be seen anywhere if the conditions are suitable, it is usually called a brockenspecter after the Brocken, a peak in the Harz mountains of Germany, where it is a familiar sight. The outline of the shadow is surrounded by a "glory," a many-colored halo of light, caused by diffraction and reflection of sunlight by the tiny water droplets of the cloud or mist. Viewers can see the glory only around their own shadow. A glory is also often seen around the shadow of an aircraft projected onto the clouds below.

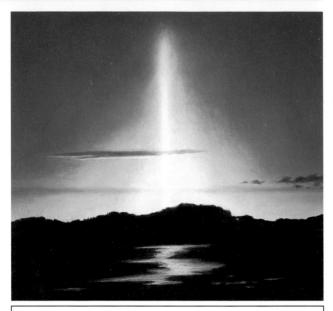

Ice crystals in the atmosphere can produce a range of optical phenomena around the Sun as a result of refraction and reflection of sunlight by the crystals. Sun pillars are vertical beams of light projecting upwards or downwards from the Sun when it is low in the sky, and are caused by reflection of sunlight from the larger ice crystals. Refraction of light through smaller prism-shaped ice crystals creates a variety of effects. The most common are solar and lunar halos, rings of light surrounding the Sun or Moon when it is veiled by a thin cloud of ice crystals (see **cirrostratus**, page 43 for illustration). The halo is usually white but may be colored, with the blue colors on the outside of the circle and the red inside. If the ice crystals orient themselves parallel to each other as they fall, the refracted rays combine to produce intense patches of light – parhelia, mock suns, or sundogs – that lie on either side of the Sun, on or just outside the radius of the halo. The icy air of the Arctic and Antarctic produces magnificent displays combining halos, mock suns, and sun pillars.

Delicately colored diffuse rings of light around the Sun or Moon are called coronas. In contrast to halos, they occur when the Sun or Moon is seen through a thin veil of water droplet cloud or mist. The droplets diffract the sunlight, bending the light rays around the droplet and causing complicated patterns of interference which create the iridescent effect.

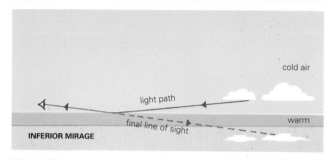

cold air

light path

warm

final line of sight

INFERIOR MIRAGE

warm air

final line of sight

light path

cold

SUPERIOR MIRAGE

Mirages are the deceptive appearance in the distance of objects that are not really there. They are caused when light coming from a distant object is refracted and reflected at the boundary between layers of cold (dense) and warm (thin) air and thus enters the eye at an unusual angle. The eye is deceived into thinking that the light is actually coming from the point at which it is looking, and so it "sees" the image there. Inferior mirages occur when there is a thin layer of very hot air at the ground surface. Light from clouds in the sky is reflected off the boundary between the hot air and colder air above it (upper illustration) and enters the eye at an angle that makes it see the image on the ground far away. The shimmering image, which is often seen in the desert or over a hot road surface, looks like a pool of water in the distance. Superior mirages are formed in cold conditions. Light from a distant object is refracted downwards at the surface of dense cold air near the ground (lower illustration) and so the eye perceives the object up in the sky. Objects below the horizon can become visible, as in the repeat sunsets seen in the Arctic and Antarctic.

AURORA

The aurora borealis or Northern Lights are often seen in latitudes
higher than 70°N, but much less frequently farther south. The
light is caused by solar discharges of atomic particles that are
trapped by the Earth's magnetic field and interact with the upper
reaches of the atmosphere to produce radiation. This can take
the form of a glow in the sky, shooting rays of light, or waving
curtains and ribbons of light. The colors vary from a vivid multi-
colored display to white. A similar spectacle, the aurora australis
or Southern Lights is visible in southern polar regions.

Thunderstorms

A severe thunderstorm is one of nature's most striking displays. The sky darkens suddenly, lightning flashes strike the ground amid torrential rain, and thunder bursts out overhead. Thunderstorms are caused by giant **cumulonimbus** clouds. Each cloud is about 3 miles across and 3 to 6 miles deep, and individual clouds may last only an hour or so. Transient thunderstorms are caused by low-based cumulonimbus clouds, which often accompany **cold fronts**, and may occur at any time of year. Longer-lasting thunderstorms usually occur at the end of the summer, when warm air rises into an unstable layer to form high-based thunderclouds. These conditions favor the continual growth of new thunderclouds as the previous ones disperse.

Gathering thunderclouds develop powerful updrafts within them and as the storm approaches, a gentle wind can be felt blowing towards the cloud or there is a short period of calm. As the thundercloud grows to full height a ferocious downdraft develops, bringing heavy rain or hail down from the frozen flattened cloud top (the anvil). The rain rarely lasts long, but can be heavy, and cloudbursts like these can cause local flooding. The downdraft of cold moist air eventually quenches the supply of warm air fueling the cloud's growth.

Lightning is produced by electrical activity within the cloud. The lightning discharge heats the air in its path; the air glows, and expands and contracts violently, setting up sound waves that we hear as thunder. The distance away of a thunderstorm can be roughly calculated by counting the time in seconds between the lightning flash and the clap of thunder. The light of the flash reaches the observer immediately whereas sound only travels at around 1100 feet ($\frac{1}{5}$ mile) per second. If the thunderstorm is a mile away you will hear the thunder about 5 seconds after you see the lightning. The rolling thunder that often follows the first sharp thunderclap is caused by echoes from clouds.

Lightning seeks out the shortest path to the ground so that isolated trees or a person out in the open are most at risk of being struck. Tall buildings like church towers and spires used to be particularly vulnerable before the invention of lightning conductors.

Lightning is the result of electrical activity in a thundercloud. Electrical charges separate within the giant cloud. The cloud top becomes positive with most other parts becoming negative. The electrical difference is resolved by powerful electrical discharges that we see as lightning. Discharges can leap from cloud to cloud or from cloud to oppositely charged patches of ground under the cloud. Because air conducts electricity badly, the "leader stroke" from cloud to ground travels quite slowly, forming a thin branched channel of ionized air which becomes visible only as the leader nears the ground. The blinding flash of forked lightning we see is the "return stroke" flashing up and down these channels from ground to cloud at high speeds (87,000 miles per second) and heating the surrounding air to immensely high temperatures (up to 100,000°F). Sheet lightning is unseen forked lightning reflected from clouds. There are many anecdotal records of another kind of lightning – ball lightning. This phenomenon, where a ball of glowing light appears and moves around, has no good scientific explanation.

WORLD CLIMATE

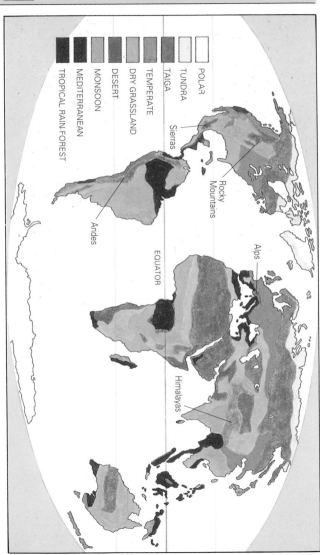

TROPICAL RAIN FOREST
MEDITERRANEAN
MONSOON
DESERT
DRY GRASSLAND
TEMPERATE
TAIGA
TUNDRA
POLAR

Sierras
Rocky Mountains
Andes
Alps
EQUATOR
Himalayas

Climate

The climate of an area is an overall description of the type of weather it can expect to have throughout the year. The main determinants of climate are temperature and rainfall and how they vary during the year. The distance from the Equator – the latitude – is one of the main influences on climate. It determines both the average temperature, and whether there are marked differences between seasons. Because the surface of the Earth is curved, the amount of solar radiation received per unit area becomes less as one moves polewards from the Equator. The area around the Equator receives most and the poles least (see **Temperature**). As the Earth is also tilted on its axis, the amount of radiation received at the poles, and in the northern and southern midlatitudes (between 40° and 60°), also varies throughout the year as the Earth makes its annual journey around the Sun. The variation in length of day and night, and differences in temperatures at different times of year give clearly marked seasons in these latitudes, each with its own seasonal weather. At the Equator, in contrast, day length and temperature are fairly constant throughout the year.

Along the same latitude, climate tends to vary with distance from the sea and whether there are high mountain ranges that create "rain-shadow" deserts behind them. Maritime regions experience less extreme variation in temperature and rainfall between winter and summer than do continental interiors because the oceans have a moderating influence. Deep water warms up and cools down much more slowly than land, and thus oceans tend to exert a cooling influence in the hottest season and are a source of heat in winter. On a more local scale, a warm ocean **current** nearby can make a region much milder than one might expect for the latitude.

Climatic zones

The combination of rainfall and temperature, and the way in which they vary throughout the year, give each climatic zone a typical vegetation, and this is how climates are often classified. On the map opposite, the main climate/vegetation zones are marked: glacial (**polar**), **tundra**, cool temperate (**taiga**), warm **temperate**, **Mediterranean**, dry grassland (**prairie**, **steppe** and savanna), the monsoon zones where rainfall is highly seasonal, **tropical rain forest**, and **desert**.

POLAR

The glacial climates of the high Arctic and Antarctic have a mean temperature in the warmest summer month of below 32°F. There is a permanent cover of snow and ice. The Arctic is an ocean of permanent pack ice surrounded by land, whereas Antarctica is an isolated land continent fringed with sea ice and surrounded by ocean. The air is cold and dry, and there is little or no precipitation. What there is falls as snow. The permanent snow cover reflects most of the Sun's radiation, helping to keep temperatures low in summer. Polar conditions also occur on the tops of high mountains outside the polar regions. At the poles themselves there is a period of around 6 months continuous daylight in "summer" and 6 months of continuous night in "winter." The harshest conditions on Earth are those of the Antarctic plateau, where the polar cold is intensified by altitude above sea level and strong winds. At the Soviet base of Vostok, over 10,700 feet above sea level, mean annual temperature is −70°F and average temperature in July (the Antarctic winter) can be as low as −126°F. Snowfall there has never been recorded.

In the Arctic, the lands surrounding the permanent polar ice pack form the tundra, a vast treeless region extending to the northern limit at which plants can grow. The mean temperature in the warmest month in summer rises above 32°F but never exceeds 50°F. This is enough, however, to melt the snow and allow plants to grow. A few feet below the surface the ground remains permanently frozen. The vegetation of lichens, moss and grass, perennial flowers and a few dwarf shrubs is adapted to make the most of the short summer, which may only last a month or two. In the winter, the persistent snow cover helps to insulate the surface vegetation from the low temperatures (down to −22° F for January). Although precipitation is low (usually less than 10 inches per year) the ground is moist as the melted snow cannot drain through the frozen layer and does not evaporate in the cool air. A similar type of vegetation is found farther south on high mountains.

To the south of the tundra lies the taiga, a zone of mainly coniferous forest mixed with hardy deciduous trees like birches and willows. It is defined by mean temperature in the warmest summer month (July) above 50°F and a mean temperature in the coldest winter month of below 26°F. It extends throughout central Scandinavia, Russia and Canada. Long, cold, dry winters are followed by a short summer. Almost all rain and snow fall between May and October, and some of the greatest extremes in the world between winter and summer temperatures are experienced in the continental interiors. A range from 86°F in July to −22°F in January is quite usual.

Temperate climates occur in the midlatitudes and are characterized by a mean temperature in the hottest month of more than 50°F and rain (or snow in winter) all the year round. In New York for example, median monthly precipitation varies between 2.7 inches in January and 3.5 inches in August, with fairly similar amounts each month. There is a great variation within this broad climatic type, between the maritime climates of the Pacific northwest coast, the more continental climate of the northeastern United States, and the subtropical monsoon-type climates of the south. Average monthly temperatures in maritime Seattle, for example, range between 40°F in January to around 65°F in August, whereas the continental Chicago ranges from 21°F in January to around 73°F in July. The natural vegetation cover for temperate Europe and the eastern United States is broad-leaved deciduous forest, now largely cleared for agriculture.

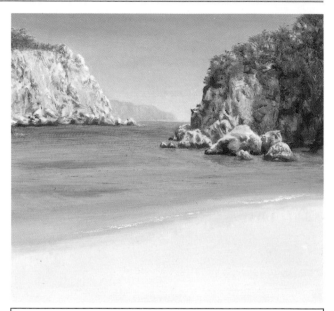

Around the Mediterranean Sea the climate is hot and dry in summer, and mild and moist in winter, with mean summer temperatures between 68°F and 80°F and winter temperatures between 40°F and 55°F. Annual rainfall is between 16 and 32 inches and falls mostly in winter, between November and March. It rarely snows, but night frosts can occur in winter. This type of climate is also found in California, parts of Chile, South Africa, and southwestern Australia. Conifers and thick-leaved evergreen trees and shrubs, which can withstand the dry summers, are the natural vegetation.

The grasslands of the Northern Hemisphere – the prairies of North America and the steppes of central Asia – occur in the continental interiors, cut off from moisture-laden winds by the mountain barrier of the Rocky Mountains on the one hand and distance from the ocean on the other. In general, severe winters with sub-zero temperatures are followed by warm or hot summers with average temperatures in the hottest month between 60° F and 80° F. With annual precipitation (snow and rain) of less than 40 inches, it is generally too dry for trees to flourish and continuous forest to develop. The natural vegetation is grass and grassland flowers. Most precipitation, however, falls as rain in the growing season, thus making some of these areas suitable for agriculture, and much of the original dry grassland of the North American prairie has been transformed into one of the main wheat-growing areas of the world. Other temperate grasslands are the veldt of southern Africa, the pampas of South America and the downs of Australia. Tropical grasslands include the savannas of Africa, between the equatorial rain forest and the Sahara.

⊕ TROPICAL RAIN FOREST

On either side of the Equator, between latitudes around 5°S and 10°N, rainfall of between 80 and 160 inches and constant temperatures of around 80°F support the luxuriant tropical rain forest. There are no marked seasons so near the Equator and growth continues throughout the year. The high rainfall comes from the **cumulus** clouds that form continually in the warm air rising at the Equator (see **General Circulation**) and **thunderstorms** are common. The main areas of tropical rain forest are in the Amazon basin of South America, central Africa, and southeast Asia, extending from Sri Lanka to Thailand and through the Philippines and Malaysia to Papua–New Guinea and the extreme northwest of Australia. Tropical rain forest is now disappearing at an alarming rate.

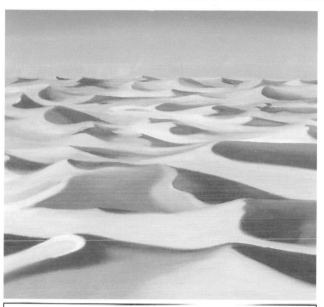

Deserts lie under areas of almost permanent atmospheric high pressure or are shielded from moist winds by high mountain barriers. Rainfall is less than 4 inches per year and erratic, and evaporates rapidly. The Atacama desert on the west coast of South America has less than ¾ inch of rain annually. This coastal strip is desert because prevailing winds blow not from the sea but from the interior, and are blocked by the Andes. Some places in the Atacama have had almost no rain for hundreds of years. Temperatures in hot deserts soar to over 104°F in daytime in summer but desert nights can be cold as the bare ground loses heat rapidly. Desert plants are adapted to conserve moisture and are succulents like cacti, spiny shrubs, or annuals which lie dormant as seeds until the rain comes. The largest desert in the world is the Sahara, with its shifting dunes of sand and the highest recorded temperature of 136°F. The main hot deserts are the central Australian desert, the Atacama, and the Kalahari in southern Africa. The Gobi desert of central Asia and the North American desert of California and Arizona are sometimes termed "cold" deserts because of their low winter temperatures.

Weather Observation

Although we grumble at the weather forecast when we get caught in an unexpected downpour, short-term weather forecasts are today probably as accurate as they can be. Local variations occur within the space of even a few miles, and if you get to know the tricks of your local weather you can often interpret the general weather forecast better.

The forecasts put out by the National Weather Service depend on gathering as much information about weather and atmospheric conditions from as many sources as possible. At set times of the day, data from individual weather stations are relayed to regional and national forecasting centers. The information is then fed into computers and rapidly plotted onto charts to give a snapshot picture of atmospheric conditions over the whole area at a particular time. As weather does not keep to national boundaries, weather centers worldwide are linked into an international network and exchange information. Once all the data have been processed, experienced meteorologists draw in isobars and **fronts** and make a forecast of the weather for a particular area for periods from a few hours to a few days ahead. Today, they are aided by some of the most powerful computers in the world, and by satellite pictures that show approaching weather systems.

Daily national and regional forecasts are released to the general public through newspapers, television, and radio, and more localized and specialized forecasts are prepared for those whose livelihood, or even their lives, depend on the weather.

The raw data on which forecasts are based come from ground-based weather stations and ships, from weather balloons carrying instruments high into the troposphere, and from satellites looking down on the Earth from space.

But you do not need a satellite to make a study of the weather yourself. You can keep a useful weather diary with just a few items of equipment. A **barometer** to measure atmospheric pressure and a maximum and minimum **thermometer** to measure temperature are essentials. A simple **rain gauge** to measure rainfall is easily constructed and the Beaufort Scale (see pages 124/125) can be used to estimate wind speed. Learn to recognize the types of clouds in the sky and to measure the amount of cloud cover by sight.

MERCURY
BAROMETER

ANEROID
BAROMETER

vacuum

open
end

31
30

0
(inches)

PRESSURE UNIT EQUIVALENTS

millibars (mb)	965	982	999	1016	1033
inches (in.)	28.5	29.0	29.5	30.0	30.5
millimeters (mm)	724	737	749	762	775

Atmospheric pressure is measured by a barometer. There are two main types – mercury and aneroid. The mercury barometer measures atmospheric pressure by the height of the column of mercury it supports. The aneroid type has an internal sealed compartment partially emptied of air with a thin corrugated lid that moves in and out as pressure changes. It is slightly less accurate than a mercury barometer but more convenient. Ignore the markings "Rain," "Change," and "Fair" which traditionally ornament the dials of household barometers. Although high pressure often goes with good weather and low pressure with bad, this is not always so, and it is the changes in pressure, rather than the absolute pressures, that will help you to forecast the weather. Unless you are at sea level, you will need to calibrate the barometer for the change in pressure with altitude, so that you can compare your readings with those given by the weather service. Your local weather center will help. Modern barometers are marked in millibars (running from around 950 to 1050 mb); older instruments will have the equivalent in inches (28 to 31) or millimeters (700 to 787) of mercury.

TEMPERATURE and HUMIDITY

MAXIMUM
THERMOMETER

WET BULB
THERMOMETER

Air temperature is measured in degrees Celsius (°C) or Fahrenheit (°F)*, by a thermometer placed in a shaded, well ventilated position outside. To shield thermometers from the heating effect of direct sunlight they are usually placed behind a "Stevenson screen," the white slatted box you see at a weather station. A north-facing wall is the best alternative for the amateur observer. An inexpensive thermometer for use in average climates is a maximum/minimum garden thermometer with which you can record the maximum daytime and minimum nighttime temperatures. In official weather recordings an alcohol thermometer is used to measure minimum temperatures as mercury freezes at −39.77°F. A mercury thermometer with the bulb covered in muslin kept damp from a water reservoir becomes a "wet-bulb" thermometer for measuring **humidity**. In dry air, water evaporates rapidly from the muslin, cooling the thermometer; in saturated air, evaporation is nonexistent and the thermometer registers the ambient air temperature. The humidity can be calculated from the difference in the readings from a "wet-bulb" and an ordinary thermometer using conversion tables.

* Conversion of °F to °C: °C = $\frac{5}{9}$ (°F − 32);   °F = (°C x $\frac{9}{5}$) + 32

RAINFALL and CLOUD COVER

As well as the barometer (usually placed indoors) and a range of thermometers housed in their Stevenson screen, a basic weather station will also include a rain gauge (**1**) for measuring rainfall. This is a metal container with a standard sized funnel opening, which is placed away from obstacles and emptied at set periods. The water is measured, and converted into millimeters or inches of rainfall – that is, the depth to which the rain (or snow) falling in a certain period would cover the ground if it did not drain away or evaporate. A homemade rain gauge is easily improvised. Cloud cover costs nothing to measure as it is assessed by eye in eighths of total sky area covered (oktas). Clear sky is reported as 0/8; completely overcast, 8/8, and half clouded, 4/8; or by symbols as depicted in the Glossary. The sky in the picture is half clouded. Scattered clouds are brought together into one mass for measurement purposes. The traditional saying that if you can see a patch of blue sky "big enough to make a Dutchman a pair of trousers" the cloud will soon disperse, is true enough for the thin layer of early morning cloud that forms in moist warm air in spring and summer.

- - - → wind at 1650 ft
———→ surface wind

An official weather station will be equipped with instruments like the cup anemometer for measuring wind speed, which is generally reported as the average speed over a 10-minute period. The anemometer is mounted on a mast together with a wind vane to show direction. A useful estimate of wind speed can be made by the amateur using the Beaufort Scale (pages 124/125). Estimating wind direction is often difficult, especially in the average urban backyard surrounded by buildings and trees. Looking at the direction in which the clouds are moving can help, but remember that, compared with the direction of clouds at around 1650 feet high, wind near the ground is deflected by friction by as much as 20° or 30° towards a center of low pressure or outward from a high pressure center. Use Buys Ballot's Law (page 83) to determine the direction in which the area of low pressure lies.

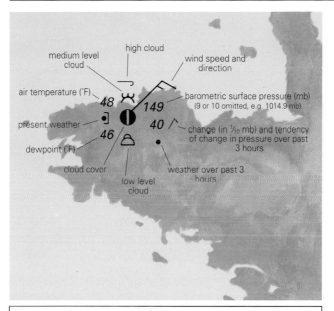

medium level cloud

high cloud

wind speed and direction

air temperature (°F)

48

149

barometric surface pressure (mb)
(9 or 10 omitted, e.g. 1014.9 mb)

present weather

40

46

change (in 1/10 mb) and tendency of change in pressure over past 3 hours

dewpoint (°F)

cloud cover

low level cloud

weather over past 3 hours

After noting temperature, pressure, and direction of change, wind direction and speed, cloud cover and cloud types, you should complete the diary by recording the actual weather for the day. Meteorologists officially distinguish a hundred or so different types of weather and weather phenomena you may encounter, from drizzle to a tornado. But you can record the weather clearly in terms of a few commonsense categories: (1) state of the sky (is it blue, partly cloudy, cloudy or overcast?); (2) precipitation (is it raining, drizzling, showery, snowing, hailing, or sleeting? And if so is precipitation light, heavy, continuous, or intermittent?); (3) electrical phenomena (are you in the middle of a thunderstorm, or can you hear distant thunder and see distant lightning?); (4) visibility (is it misty, hazy, foggy); and (5) ground phenomena (dew, hoar frost). The illustration shows how the state of the weather and atmospheric conditions at certain time are summarized on weather station records using internationally agreed symbols (see Glossary).

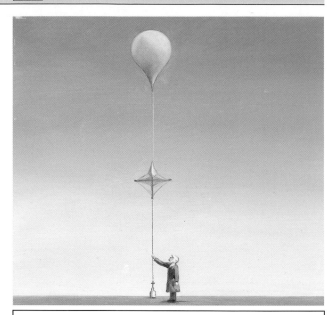

Observations at ground-level can only give part of the weather picture. To make accurate forecasts meteorologists also need to know what atmospheric conditions are like higher up. Weather balloons carry instruments up to altitudes of 22 miles to measure temperature, pressure and humidity. The information is relayed continuously to the ground by radio signals. Our knowledge of world weather has also been transformed by satellites. Geostationary satellites, some 24,000 miles above the Equator, move over it at the same speed as the Earth's rotation and so view the same area continuously. Polar orbiting satellites circle the Earth from pole to pole at around 520 miles high, taking 100 minutes to complete an orbit. They observe a band of the Earth's surface around 1850 miles wide at each orbit and cover the whole of the globe in 24 hours as it rotates beneath them, relaying a continuous picture which is picked up in turn by receiving stations around the globe. Satellites give a bird's-eye view of weather systems and are especially valuable for scanning the oceans, the poles, and the tropics where surface measurements are scarce.

UPPER AIR CHART

In order to forecast the weather at the Earth's surface accurately, meteorologists need to construct pressure and air movement charts of the upper air as well as the surface. The illustration shows a so-called 500 mb chart that corresponds to the surface chart on page 31. The 500 mb map is constructed by plotting the contours of altitude where atmospheric pressure equals 500 mb. At these altitudes, the general westward airflow over the North American continent becomes much more obvious.

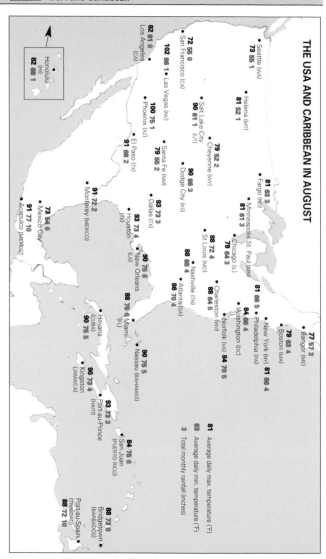

THE USA AND CARIBBEAN IN AUGUST

Seattle (WA) **73 55 1**

Helena (MT) **81 52 1**

San Francisco (CA) **72 55 0**

Las Vegas (NV) **102 66 1**

Los Angeles (CA) **82 61 0**

Salt Lake City (UT) **90 61 1**

Phoenix (AZ) **100 75 1**

El Paso (TX) **91 68 2**

Santa Fe (NM) **79 55 2**

Cheyenne (WY) **79 52 2**

Dodge City (KS) **90 66 3**

Fargo (ND) **81 63 3**

Minneapolis St. Paul (MN) **81 61 3**

Chicago (IL) **79 64 3**

St. Louis (MO) **88 72 4**

Dallas (TX) **93 73 3**

Houston (TX) **93 74 4**

New Orleans (LA) **90 75 6**

Nashville (TN) **88 68 4**

Atlanta (GA) **86 70 4**

Charleston (WV) **88 64 5**

Norfolk (VA) **84 70 5**

Washington (DC) **84 66 4**

Philadelphia (PA) **81 66 5**

New York (NY) **81 66 4**

Boston (MA) **79 63 4**

Bangor (ME) **77 57 3**

Miami (FL) **88 76 6**

Nassau (BAHAMAS) **90 75 5**

Havana (CUBA) **90 75 5**

Kingston (JAMAICA) **90 73 4**

Port-au-Prince (HAITI) **93 73 3**

San Juan (PUERTO RICO) **84 76 6**

Bridgetown (BARBADOS) **88 73 6**

Port-of-Spain (TRINIDAD) **88 72 10**

Monterey (MEXICO) **91 72 2**

Mexico City (MEXICO) **73 54 6**

Acapulco (MEXICO) **91 77 10**

Honolulu (HI) **82 68 1**

81 Average daily max. temperature (°F)

63 Average daily min. temperature (°F)

3 Total monthly rainfall (inches)

VACATION WEATHER
Europe

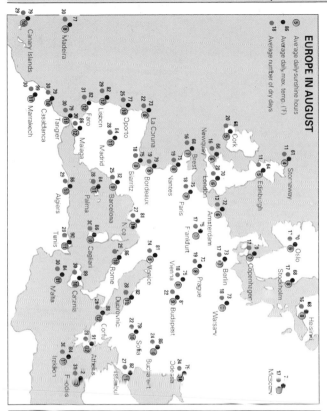

EUROPE IN AUGUST

- ⑤ Average daily sunshine hours
- 86 Average daily max. temp. (°F)
- 18 Average number of dry days

Canary Islands 79 ⑩ 29
Madeira 86 ⑧ 30
Marrakech 99 ⑪ 30
Casablanca 79 ⑩ 30
Tangier 82 ⑫ 29 / 30 ⑩ 31
Faro 82 ⑫ / 86 ⑪ 30 / 79 ⑩
Lisbon 79 ⑪ 25
Malaga 84 ⑪
Oporto 77 ⑩ 22
Madrid 84 ⑪ 28
La Coruña 73 ⑧ 16
Algiers 86 ⑪ 29
Biarritz 73 ⑧ 25
Bordeaux 79 ⑨ 18
Palma 84 ⑪ 28
Barcelona 84 ⑪ 32
Nantes 75 ⑧ 18
Brest 68 ⑥ 16
Newquay 66 ⑥ 20
Cork 66 ⑤ 68
Stornaway 61 ④ 11
London 72 ⑥ 13
Paris 75 ⑧ 19
Tunis 88 23
Cagliari 86 ⑩ 26
Rome 86 ⑩ 30
Catania 84 ⑩ 30
Malta 30 ⑩ 84
Venice 81 ⑦ 34
Frankfurt 75 ⑦ 17
Amsterdam 71 ⑤ 17
Edinburgh 64 ⑤ 11
Vienna 75 ⑧ 19
Prague 72 ⑥ 18
Berlin 73 ⑦ 17
Copenhagen 70 ⑦ 18
Oslo 70 ①
Stockholm 68 17
Helsinki 68 ⑧ 16
Moscow 7 ⑤ 17
Budapest 82 ⑨ 17
Warsaw 73 ⑧ 18
Dubrovnik 82 28
Corfu 88 ⑫ 23
Sofia 79 ⑨ 22
Athens 91 ⑪ 29
Istanbul 82 ⑨ 27
Bucharest 84 ⑨ 24
Odessa 75 ⑤ 26
Rhodes 86 ⑫ 31 / 2 ③

Data collected over many years can be analyzed to give the average weather conditions for a city or region, which can be helpful when planning a vacation or business trip. The map on page 120 shows average maximum and minimum temperatures, and the average monthly rainfall for locations in the United States and Caribbean for the month of August. The map on page 121 shows maximum daily temperature, average number of hours of sunshine daily, and average number of dry days, for the principal European cities and vacation destinations for the same month.

The map on p. 121 is published by permission of the UK Met. Office

Index

The Beaufort Scale

Force	Description	Sea state	Effects on land	Speed (miles per hour)
0	Calm	Sea like mirror	No wind; smoke rises vertically	<1
1	Light air	Ripples with appearance of scales; no foam crests	No noticeable wind; vanes remain still but smoke drifts	1–3
2	Light breeze	Wavelets, small but pronounced; glassy crests do not break	Wind felt on face; vanes move, leaves rustle	4–7
3	Gentle breeze	Large wavelets; crests begin to break; glassy foam; occasional white horses	Hair and clothing disturbed; light flag extended; leaves and small twigs move constantly	8–12
4	Moderate breeze	Small waves becoming longer; frequent white horses	Hair disarranged; raises dust and loose paper; moves small branches	13–18
5	Fresh breeze	Moderate waves of long form; many white horses; some spray	Disagreeable wind, force felt on body; small trees in leaf begin to sway	19–24
6	Strong breeze	Some large waves; extensive white foam crests and some spray	Difficult to walk steadily; umbrellas hard to control; large branches move; telegraph wires whistle	25–31
7	Moderate gale	Sea heaped up; white foam from breaking waves blowing in streaks	Some resistance to walking; whole trees move	32–38

8	Fresh gale	Moderately high and long waves; crests break into spindrift, blowing foam in well-marked streaks	Impedes progress; breaks twigs off trees	39–46
9	Strong gale	High waves; dense foam streaks in wind; wave crests topple, tumble and roll over; spray reduces visibility	People blown over by gusts; removes roof tiles and chimney-pots	47–54
10	Whole gale	Very high waves with overhanging crests; dense, blowing foam; sea surface appears white; heavy tumbling of sea, shock-like poor visibility	Rare inland; trees uprooted; much structural damage	55–63
11	Storm	Exceptionally high waves, sometimes concealing small and medium-sized ships; sea completely covered with long white patches of foam; edges of wave crests blown into froth; poor visibility	Rare; widespread damage	64–72
12	Hurricane	Air filled with foam and spray; sea white with driving spray; visibility bad	Rare	>72

125